IS THE U.S. TRADE DEFICIT SUSTAINABLE?

CATHERINE L. MANN

IS THE U.S. TRADE DEFICIT SUSTAINABLE?

INSTITUTE FOR INTERNATIONAL ECONOMICS
Washington, DC
September 1999

Catherine L. Mann, *Senior Fellow,* held several posts at the Federal Reserve Board of Governors (1984-87 and 1989-97), including Assistant Director and Special Assistant to the Staff Director, International Finance Division (1994-97). She was a Senior Economist on the Staff of the President's Council of Economic Advisers (1991-92), the principal staff member for the Chief Economists of the World Bank (1988-89), and a Ford Foundation Fellow at the National Bureau of Economic Research (1987). She is an Adjunct Professor at the Owen School of Management at Vanderbilt University and has also taught at the University of Chicago, Princeton University, University of Maryland, Georgetown University, Boston College, and Massachusetts Institute of Technology. She has written numerous articles on international trade and finance, publishing in the *American Economic Review, Journal of International Money and Finance, Brookings Papers on Economic Activity,* and *International Economy,* among other journals and volumes. She is coauthor and coeditor of *Evaluating Policy Regimes.*

INSTITUTE FOR INTERNATIONAL ECONOMICS
11 Dupont Circle, NW
Washington, DC 20036-1207
(202) 328-9000   FAX: (202) 328-5432
http://www.iie.com

C. Fred Bergsten, *Director*
Christine R. Flint, *Director of Publications*
Brett Kitchen, *Marketing Director*

Typesetting by BMWW
Printing by Automated Graphic Systems

Printed in the United States of America
01 00 99   5 4 3 2 1

Library of Congress Cataloging-in-Publication Data

Mann, Catherine L.
    Is the U.S. trade deficit sustainable? / Catherine L. Mann.
        p. cm.
    Includes bibliographical references and index.
    ISBN 0-88132-265-2

    1. Balance of trade—United States.
    2. United States—Commerce.
    3. International trade.   4. Competition, International.   5. United States—Commercial policy.   6. United States—Foreign economic relations.   I. Title: Is the US trade deficit sustainable?
HF3031.M275   1999
382'.17'0973—dc21   99-31295
                                                     CIP

Contents

Tables

Figures

Preface

The Institute has conducted extensive research over the years on the current account deficit of the United States, its sustainability in both financial and trade policy terms, and its impact on the world economy as a whole. *Deficits and the Dollar: The World Economy at Risk* by Stephen Marris in 1985 was called "the *locus classicus* of the hard landing scenario" by *The Economist*. My *America in the World Economy* in 1988 stressed the need for the United States to correct the "twin deficits" of that period. *American Trade Adjustment: The Global Impact* by William R. Cline in 1989 quantified the changes required to achieve such adjustment and the effects on other key countries. *Has the Adjustment Process Worked?* by Paul Krugman in 1991 assessed the results of the policy initiatives undertaken in the 1980s, with country details provided in my edited volume *International Adjustment and Financing: The Lessons of 1985-91* (1991).

A particular emphasis of Institute research has been the level of exchange rates, for the dollar and other currencies, needed to achieve and maintain international equilibrium. John Williamson pioneered the concept of "fundamental equilibrium exchange rates," based on sustainable current account positions, in *The Exchange Rate System* (1983) and updated his calculations in *Estimating Equilibrium Exchange Rates* (1994). Complementary estimates were derived by Cline in *Predicting External Imbalances for the United States and Japan* (1995). Simon Wren-Lewis and Rebecca Driver provided the most recent updates in *Real Exchange Rates for the Year 2000* (1998).

This new study by Catherine L. Mann takes a fresh look at all these issues. It places the record US trade and current account deficits of 1999 squarely in the context of America's dramatic economic progress in the 1990s and its overall position in the world economy. It takes full account of the enormous changes that have occurred since the United States ran its previous record deficits in the middle 1980s, both in America's own economic situation and in the global capital markets that provide external financing for the United States. It analyzes the intensive global interactions both within and between real economies as well as the financial and trade policy dimensions of the current account issue.

Dr. Mann's conclusions are both hopeful and sobering. She believes that the current account imbalance is financially sustainable "for two or three more years," and sees a prospect for long-term resolution of the problem through a rise in household savings in the United States and further opening of foreign markets to exports from America's highly competitive services sector. On the other hand, she notes that trade politics in the United States are already moving in an unhealthy direction, partly due to the external deficit; that the present rate of buildup of the country's foreign debt will become unsustainable at some fairly early point; and that a sharp fall of the dollar, while the economy is still operating near full capacity, could be quite costly and complicate policymaking considerably. We hope that her study will both enhance public understanding of an unusually complex issue and offer practical suggestions for constructive policy responses to it.

The Institute for International Economics is a private nonprofit institution for the study and discussion of international economic policy. Its purpose is to analyze important issues in that area and to develop and communicate practical new approaches for dealing with them. The Institute is completely nonpartisan.

The Institute is funded largely by philanthropic foundations and private corporations. Major institutional grants are now being received from The German Marshall Fund of the United States, which created the Institute with a generous commitment of funds in 1981, from The William M. Keck, Jr. Foundation and from The Starr Foundation. A number of other foundations and companies also contribute to the highly diversified financial resources of the Institute. About 18 percent of the Institute's resources in our latest fiscal year were provided by contributors outside the United States, including about 12 percent from Japan.

Partial funding for this project was provided by the Toyota Motor Corporation under the Institute's new program of studies on the backlash against globalization, a topic of central interest in both the United States and Japan. The program was created in 1998 to analyze the nature and significance of the backlash, and the resultant need for improved understanding of both globalization itself and policy responses that can improve its contribution to the world economy. Support for this program is also being provided by Stephan Schmidheiny, a Director of the Institute, who has helped shape our research program as well as provided generous funding for it.

The Board of Directors bears overall responsibility for the Institute and gives general guidance and approval to its research program—including identification of topics that are likely to become important to international economic policymakers over the medium run (generally, one to three years), and which thus should be addressed by the Institute. The Director, working closely with the staff and outside Advisory Committee, is responsible for the development of particular projects and makes the final decision to publish an individual study.

The Institute hopes that its studies and other activities will contribute to building a stronger foundation for international economic policy around the world. We invite readers of these publications to let us know how they think we can best accomplish this objective.

C. FRED BERGSTEN
Director
August 1999

Acknowledgments

A key indicator of an interesting book topic is how many people are willing to read drafts of the whole text—in some cases more than once! I hope I have not let any of them down. I particularly appreciate the efforts of C. Fred Bergsten, Robert A. Blecker, Richard N. Cooper, I. M. Destler, Barry Eichengreen, Jessica P. Einhorn, William L. Helkie, Peter Hooper, Karen H. Johnson, Stephen Marris, Gerald A. Pollak, and Obie G. Whichard, who helped me enormously in improving the volume. In addition, active participation at study groups by my colleagues at the Institute and by Ralph Bryant, Tom Dorsey, Timothy Duy, Isaiah Frank, Kent Hughes, Jeri Jensen-Moran, Robert Lawrence, Thea Lee, Marcus Miller, and Charles P. Thomas helped me to hone the content. Hiroki Ishii was a tremendous research assistant for the bulk of the book, and Erika Wada helped in finalizing the work. John J. Guardiano used a editorial light hand on the text, and also employed his artistic talents in polishing the manuscript. Finally, I would like to single out for special thanks Ted Truman, my colleague while we were both at the Federal Reserve, whose demand for clear thinking, analytical detail, and honest exposition underpin this work. All told, I have received much assistance in the preparation of the volume, though I alone am responsible for the views expressed here and the errors that remain.

1

Introduction

1980s Redux?

Forecasters project that the US trade deficit in 1999 will reach about $200 billion, and the current account deficit will be more than $300 billion, or about 3.3 percent of GDP. The trajectory for the year 2000 and beyond exhibits further widening. The current account deficit has not been this large in percentage terms since 1987, when the trade deficit was $153 billion and the current account deficit $170 billion.

The US economy is expected to continue to outperform the rest of the world in 1999, with an expected GDP growth of at least 3.5 percent, compared to the industrial countries' average of around 2 percent. This divergence in growth rates is eerily similar to what we saw in the mid-1980s, when the United States rebounded from the 1981-82 global recession much more quickly than did its industrial-country trading partners.

The exchange value of the dollar appreciates in response to the higher actual and expected returns that come with robust growth. Accordingly, between 1981 and 1985, the exchange value of the dollar appreciated some 50 percent against the currencies of the major US trading partners. Between mid-1995 and early 1998 the dollar also appreciated, although by a more modest 25 percent.

Along with these similarities between the two periods, might there be another forthcoming? After its substantial run-up, between 1985 and 1987 the dollar depreciated about 50 percent. While it is never easy to explain the behavior of foreign exchange markets, by February 1985 investors' and policymakers' views about the dollar complemented one another.

Table 1.1 Domestic economic indicators

	1991	1999 or latest	
GDP growth (chained 1992 $, percentage)	–0.9	4.5	(1st quarter, annualized)
Unemployment rate (percentage)	6.8	4.2	(March)
Number of employed persons (millions)	118	133	(March)
Inflation rate (CPI-urban)	3.1	1.7	(March)
Dow Jones industrial average	2,929	10,813	(1 May)
30-year US Treasury bond rate (percentage)	8.14	5.58	(1 May)
3-month US Treasury bill rate (percentage)	5.42	4.34	(1 May)
Federal budget position as percentage of GDP	–4.6	0.8	(1998)

Source: Council of Economic Advisers, *Economic Indicators* (April 1999).

Foreign investors had overbought dollars and US investments and had grown concerned about the magnitude of the external deficits and what they implied about future returns on US dollar investments. Policymakers, too, were alarmed at the value of the dollar and of their own currencies, and agreed in the context of the Plaza Agreement and later the Louvre Accord to undertake joint intervention in the foreign exchange markets to encourage the dollar down and then to maintain it at what they considered a more sustainable rate.

As we consider the constellation of domestic and external economic data for the United States and the world in 1999 and 2000, does a significant depreciation of the dollar appear inevitable? Or are the external deficits more sustainable now than they were in the mid-1980s, given that the US economy is different and that the factors underlying the widening of the deficits in the 1990s are different from those of the 1980s? More generally, once such large imbalances emerge, what factors can help to right them in an orderly way?

The US Economy in the 1990s: Robust Domestic Growth and Rapid Global Integration

Through the 1990s, US economic performance strengthened, to the envy of the world (table 1.1). The United States is the undisputed technological leader. The government budget is in surplus. Some 133 million people are now employed, and the unemployment rate has fallen below 4.5 percent, the lowest in a generation. At the same time, inflation has fallen and remains under 2 percent, also the lowest in three decades. During this expansion, US corporations have generated unprecedented wealth, which is

Table 1.2 External economic indicators

	1991	1998 or latest
Exports, goods and services (billions of US dollars)	601.8	959.0
Imports, goods and services (billions of US dollars)	622.3	1,102.0
(Exports + imports)/GDP (chained 1992 $, percentage)	20	29
Capital inflows + capital outflows (billions of US dollars)	167.5	847.9[a]
Current account (billions of US dollars)	−5.7	−233.4[a]
Current account/GDP (percentage)	−0.1	−2.7
Net international investment position (current cost, billions of US dollars)	−326	−1,500[b]
Net investment receipts or payments (billions of US dollars)	21.5	−22.5[a]

a. Preliminary.
b. Estimate based on 1997 data plus 1998 current account.

Source: Council of Economic Advisers, *Economic Indicators* (April 1999).

distributed more widely across American households than ever before. Even in the face of global financial volatility and downturns in the economies of virtually all US trading partners in 1998, the US economy has continued to grow in 1999 with unprecedented robustness.

This unrivaled good news on the domestic front has been associated with a rising interdependence of the US economy with the rest of the world through trade and financial links (table 1.2). Ongoing liberalization in trade and investment policies and deregulation in telecommunications and transport promote an increasing globalization of production and distribution of goods and services. During the 1990s, exports and imports of goods and services increased some 60 and 80 percent, respectively. About 30 percent of real GDP is directly affected by the forces of international trade, with the exposure of some sectors much higher, and others affected indirectly.

The United States and, more importantly, other countries liberalized their financial systems, and US financial intermediaries helped US and foreign investors diversify their portfolios of wealth into nondomestic stocks and bonds. Net cross-border flows of capital more than quadrupled, and gross cross-border flows of financial assets amount to trillions of dollars and continue to increase.

During the 1990s the US current account, which is the broadest measure of the net flow of trade and investment income, moved from near balance to a deficit of $233 billion dollars in 1998, representing a change from zero to 2.7 percent of GDP. The deficit comes from a large and widening deficit of trade in goods, even as trade in services increasingly is in surplus.

The flip side of a trade deficit is net capital inflows. If imports are not paid for with exports, they must be paid for through net sales of domestic assets or a buildup of liabilities to foreigners. The accumulation of the flow of net investment by foreigners constitutes the US net international investment position. Whatever measurement techniques are used, the value of foreign assets owned by the United States is less than the value of US assets held by foreigners; the negative net international investment position is some $1.5 trillion dollars, about 18 percent of GDP. Over a period of less than 10 years, the net investment earnings on this position turned from a positive $22 billion to a negative $22 billion.

Global Financial Crises Highlight the Linkages

The effects of economic turmoil in many countries around the world in 1997 and 1998 highlight the growing importance of trade and financial interrelationships between the United States and the rest of the world. As the economies of Asia collapsed, as Japan's recession worsened, and as economic activity in Latin America slowed, US export growth tumbled from about 10 percent in 1997 to zero in 1998, and exports shrank in absolute terms in the early months of 1999.

At the same time, in the volatile global investment environment, particularly after Russia defaulted on its financial obligations, US securities looked especially safe and valuable. Net purchases of US government securities surged, and the 30-year bond yield dropped from 6.6 percent in mid-1997 to about 5 percent in December 1998. (As the global crises ebbed, the rate ticked back up to 6 percent.) Home mortgage rates fell in tandem, to levels not seen since the 1960s, spurring residential investment at an unprecedented pace. The Dow Jones industrial average wobbled only slightly during the turmoil before continuing its upward march, passing the 10,000 mark by early 1999.[1]

Where To from Here?
An Ever-Widening Trade Deficit?

The global financial crises will pass. Global integration will continue. Exports and imports will both increase, and investors in the United States and elsewhere will continue to diversify their financial portfolios by purchasing and selling financial assets and companies in each other's countries. National economic well-being increasingly relies on global production, distribution, consumption, and the web of international financial transactions that binds them all together.

For at least the next year or two, however, the US current account deficit will continue to grow, for two reasons: first and foremost, the trade deficit

---

1. The contrasting effect of the Asian financial crises on the US external sector (a deterioration) and the "nontraded" interest-sensitive sectors (a strengthening) is borne out by global econometric analysis in Noland, Robinson, Wang (1999).

itself, and second—and increasingly important as time goes on—the rising investment-service payments on the accumulation of nearly 20 years of deficits. The growth rate of exports will rise once growth resumes abroad, and the growth in imports will slow as the US economy returns to a growth path consistent with estimates of potential. But because the trade deficit is so large now, to actually narrow the gap between exports and imports will require a dramatic change in the growth differential, with import growth slowing markedly (to about one-quarter the average rate of growth in the 1990s) and export growth rising significantly (to about four times the rate of growth in the 1990s). Such a rapid change in the growth differential has occurred only rarely, and it could be associated with difficult economic adjustments in the United States. Second, the net investment payments on the US international investment position will continue to grow so long as the current account is in deficit and net foreign investment continues; these payments add to the negative net investment position. Hence, changing the direction of the US external balance is not a simple process.

The global financial crises and the widening US external deficits have precipitated fresh inquiry into a set of perennial questions about global integration and the US economy, which receive greater scrutiny as observers start to question the "sustainability" of the trade deficit. These questions can be structured thematically into four broad areas: (1) the forces that drive international trade, finance, and the external deficit; (2) the costs and benefits of increasing integration into the global economy; (3) the role of competitiveness and trade policy in the composition, level, and balance of trade in goods, services, and financial assets; and (4) the sustainability of the US imbalances.

My objective in this book is to provide facts and analyses in these areas and to focus attention on what should be and what should not be policy concerns, and on what actions policymakers can take, and what actions they should avoid.

Among my main points are that the trade deficit represents mostly good news—for both the United States and the rest of the world. It can continue on its current trajectory for two or three more years. Indeed, increased productivity growth associated with the globalization of production and distribution makes it possible for the imbalances to grow larger and to be sustained for a longer time than was the case in the 1980s. Moreover, the liberalization and globalization of international financial markets and institutions makes it easier and more attractive for investors to diversify their wealth portfolios to include high-return, relatively safe US investments. But the United States cannot forever consume beyond its long-term means; nor will its financial investments always be so favored.

There are some structural issues that US policymakers should face—particularly now, when the economic climate is so good. Household savings rates are too low given reasonable expectations for future income and wealth. Current and future worker preparedness for current and future jobs is inadequate and worsening. Trade negotiations must resume and should focus on multilateral liberalization of services. These structural issues facing the United States are not new, but they become more salient as the United States increasingly engages in a globalized and technology-driven marketplace.

A most important concern is the continued cyclical economic doldrums of the rest of the world. The lost decade in Japan, the tepid growth in most of Europe's economies, the tentative rebound in Asia, and the teetering of Latin America could be setting the stage for a rerun of the 1980s. If sustained growth around the world is delayed for several more years, US investments will continue to yield expected returns higher than those abroad and the dollar will continue to strengthen and the trade deficit to worsen, until a replay of 1985 for policymakers and the exchange value of the dollar becomes inevitable.

Overview and Organization of the Book

This book is designed to answer questions that policymakers often ask about US trade and foreign investment. Ten specific questions are collected around four themes.

The chapters in Part 1 address the forces that drive international trade, finance, and the external deficit. These chapters provide the framework for answering the question of what happened to the twin deficits of 1985 and of how the composition of trade and finance has changed over time. This information is important for understanding why policymakers should focus on policies to increase household savings and to promote service-sector negotiations. It also lays the groundwork for discussions on why capital flows are important when considering the sustainability of "the" deficit.

The chapters in Part 2 cover how the increasing integration into the global economy should affect policymakers' response to the external deficit. They address whether and how trade deficits hurt US workers and firms as well as how globalization is associated with increased productivity and lower inflation in the US economy. These chapters are designed in part to help policymakers counter the protectionist demands that inevitably accompany growing trade deficits, making clear that a policy partnership between government, business, unions, schools, and individuals to help firms and workers grasp new employment opportunities is required to obtain the full benefits of globalization and productivity growth. In addition, the fact that globalization and productivity growth are related implies that a larger current account deficit can be absorbed for longer now than in 1985, because the wherewithal to make good on commitments is growing.

The chapters in Part 3 consider how competitiveness and trade policy might affect the deficit and how policymakers should respond. These chapters explore the tensions between the microeconomic concept of relative price competitiveness and the macroeconomic concept of competitiveness as measured by share of global trade or by the external balance. The discussions in these chapters can help policymakers understand the long-run effects of labor quality and labor productivity on price competitiveness as well as the short- and medium-run effects of exchange rate misalignments on relative price competitiveness and trade balance. Part 3 also addresses whether and through what channels market-access negotiations with particular countries or unfair trade practices of individual countries can affect external balance. This information is designed to arm policymakers with an understanding of what bilateral deficits mean and what they do not mean, and it can help focus attention on what sorts of trade negotiations might yield the greatest improvement in external balance.

The chapters in Part 4, finally, address the question of whether the imbalances are sustainable from both the internal and external perspectives. These chapters discuss cyclical vs. structural trade deficits as well as the question of whether some trade deficits are nonproblematic in the sense that they have within them the means to finance repayment of borrowed funds or make good on expectations to return equity value. This analysis can clarify for policymakers how much of the widening of the trade deficit is associated with good US economic performance combined with poor economic performance in Japan and Europe, as well as with the fallout from the global financial crises. But it also points out that the composition of the external deficit and domestic spending (between consumption and investment) are important for ensuring that the deficit can continue to be financed. These chapters also address the relationship between capital flows and the current account.

The final chapter in Part 4 addresses the question of whether the United States is "special" and as such unlikely to suffer the fate of, say, the United Kingdom, Italy, Mexico, Russia, Brazil, or the Asian economies when investor sentiment changes. This chapter responds directly to the question of whether the trade deficit is sustainable, assessing the issue both from the standpoint of the ratio of current account to GDP and from that of capital flows as a share of global wealth.

Conclusions and Policy Recommendations

The conclusions and policy recommendations in this book are derived from complex and in-depth economic analysis of data and assessment of internal and external forces. Yet they can be summarized rather briefly. A key theme is that the globalization of the US economy blurs the traditional distinction between "trade" policy and "domestic" policy. Good policy reflects the marriage of both external and domestic needs and objectives.

■ International forces are allowing the current robust expansion to continue and are enhancing the long-term ability of the United States to grow without generating inflation. Lower inflation rates benefit all people, especially those who consume a large fraction of their income. Faster productivity growth is the foundation for higher wages and allows monetary policymakers to keep interest rates low for longer periods without having to be concerned about higher inflation rates. Hence restricting trade would negatively affect both the short-run and the long-run performance of the US economy.

■ As a general proposition, we need to describe and better quantify the benefits of globalization, since these have not been wholly understood by the population at large nor widely embraced by their elected representatives. Yet concerns over globalization are also justified, because adjustment by firms and workers to economic dynamics can be difficult and costly. The policy approach that must emerge places emphasis squarely on education and skill-training and on the creativity and flexibility of workers and management so that they can take advantage of business and job opportunities in the expanding sectors. Only a policy partnership between government, business, unions, schools, and the individual will create the kind of environment in which everyone can benefit from globalization.

■ The global financial crises and the robust US economy in combination dramatically widened the US external account deficits in 1998 and 1999. Yet, because the United States is both special and a critical participant in the international markets, the external situation is not yet unsustainable. Robust domestic demand in the United States can continue to support the resumption of global growth for two or three more years. But, because of structural asymmetries in the components of the US internal and external balance as well as political and market sensitivities to ever-increasing trade deficits, the economic forces that underpin a sustainability episode will build throughout that time frame. The key issue is how best to keep these forces at bay.

■ A significant depreciation of the dollar would keep the external accounts in sustainable territory for the near and medium terms, but would not put them on a sustainable trajectory for the long term. Without structural changes (such as raising the household savings rate, improving education for the future, and liberalizing global trade in services), a once-and-for-all depreciation of the dollar continues the cycle whereby a depreciation narrows the trade deficit initially but is followed by a widening current account deficit as structural instabilities and net investment payments take hold of the dynamics. Moreover, in the current robust economic environment, it would be difficult for the US economy to produce the additional goods and services without raising the risk of inflation and a monetary policy response that would slow the economy. Nevertheless, because an exchange rate change has a dramatic impact in the near term, it could serve to bolster political sustainability while longer-term structural initiatives pan out.

- On the agenda for structural change, the United States should push hard in the multilateral and broad-based trade negotiating round for liberalizing services. The United States has global comparative advantage in services, and services remain highly protected abroad. As economies grow, they tend to consume more services, and as income in a foreign economy grows, its imports of US services tend to rise disproportionately. Successful broad-based negotiations on trade in services will likely increase US exports of services even further, with a positive effect on the trade deficit. The long-term trajectory of the US external balances could be altered significantly by the combination of successful service-sector negotiations and broad-based liberalization and deregulation at home and especially abroad. These together would unleash higher productivity and faster growth at home and abroad, which would narrow the US current account deficit.

- An important structural link between the external balance and the internal balance is the household savings rate. The current rate of household consumption is not sustainable, and the high import intensity of US consumption is contributing to the trend deterioration of the external deficit. Current rates of household savings (even if underestimated for various reasons) have been trending downward for some time, even before the stock market began its rapid rise. When the stock market boom ebbs and when a domestic slowdown occurs, consumers are likely to increase debt burdens in order to maintain the higher consumption levels to which they have become accustomed. To the extent that today's consumption and savings profiles are driven substantially by volatile capital gains, they are not sustainable.

- For a whole host of reasons, the economies of the rest of the world need to grow more rapidly. But simply from the narrow objective of the sustainability of the current constellation of US growth and value of the dollar, if other countries grew, the rate of return to their investments would rise and the US dollar would depreciate as investors mix their portfolio of international assets instead of overweighting toward US and dollar-denominated securities. Faster growth abroad and a drifting down of the dollar would naturally help to close the US current account gap. But the longer the growth of the rest of the world stagnates or remains slow, the longer foreign investors will choose US dollar-denominated assets and keep the dollar high, and the greater the chances that an unpleasant change in investor sentiment will affect the dollar, the United States, and the world.

What Forces Drive International Trade, Finance, and the External Deficit?

2

Whatever Happened to the "Twin Deficits"?

One of the central goals of [the new (1989) administration's] economic policy should . . . be to eliminate the current account deficit. . . . The only assured and constructive means to achieve these results is for the United States to eliminate the federal government's structural budget deficit. . . .

—C. Fred Bergsten, *America in the World Economy: A Strategy for the 1990s* (1988)

[T]he growth of the U.S. trade deficit in the 1980s primarily reflects the influence of several interrelated macroeconomic developments. . . . Growth of U.S. spending relative to production and income implied a deterioration in the national saving-investment balance, which, in turn, owed much to the persistence of a large Federal deficit. . . .

—Council of Economic Advisers, *Economic Report of the President* (1988)

From 1980 to 1986, the federal budget deficit increased from 2.7 percent of GDP to 5 percent of GDP ($220 billion) and the current account deficit increased from 0 to 3.5 percent of GDP ($153 billion). The two were called the "twin deficits" because they increased about the same amount and they derived from some of the same economic fundamentals.

Many policymakers and economists were concerned about both deficits, in part because each implied a growing debt burden and growing investment-service payments. The current account deficit was a particular concern, because investment-service payments go abroad (instead of

Figure 2.1 The twin deficits: A perspective from the times

percentage of GDP

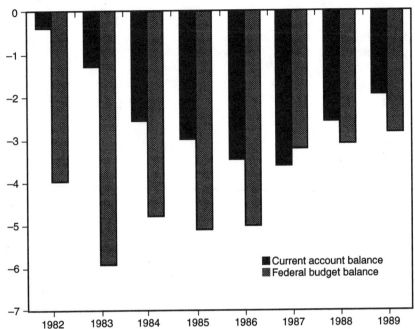

Sources: US Department of Commerce, *International Transactions Tables;* Council of Economic Advisers, *Economic Report of the President.*

immediately back into the domestic economy). Moreover, as the external deficit continued to grow and add to the value of external obligations, policymakers were concerned that participants in international financial markets might flee dollar assets and precipitate a crash of the dollar if they suddenly decided that the United States owed foreign investors too much (see, for example, Marris 1985).

Policymakers had at their disposal clear legislative channels to reduce the federal budget deficit: Reduce spending or raise taxes. These legislative policies also work through changing private-sector behavior to affect the external balance, but many people thought that the most direct way to reduce the current account deficit was to reduce the federal budget deficit.

Of course, during the 1990s the federal budget deficit has been brought to zero, but the current account deficit generally has trended toward a larger negative number, reaching $233 billion in 1998, or 2.7 percent of GDP. Why were the two deficits linked in the 1980s—and what separated them in the 1990s?

Why Were the Two Deficits Thought to Be Twins?

Several ways of inspecting the data and approaching analysis supported the twin-deficits hypothesis—including simply plotting the course of the two deficits over time (figure 2.1), in which they appeared to move together. More compelling, however, was the support found in analysis using the national income and product accounts (NIPA) framework and in the analysis of economic relationships common to the two deficits. Collectively these comprised what appeared to be a strong case for linkage.

Accounting Identities Supported Their Relationship

The twin-deficits hypothesis was embodied in the accounting relationships of the national income and product accounts framework. The NIPA framework decomposes national income (Y, which is equal to domestic production, that is, GDP) into macroeconomic aggregates that correspond to important groups of spenders in the economy: consumer household spending (C), business investment spending on equipment, facilities, and inventory (I), government spending (G), spending by foreigners on domestically produced goods and services (exports, X), and spending by domestic households, businesses, and government on foreign-produced goods and services (imports, M).[1]

The NIPA framework can be rearranged to highlight the relationship between the fiscal budget and the current account. In any economy, total savings finances investment (S = I). Total savings in an economy has three components: the amount saved by the private sector, the amount saved by the public sector, and the amount saved by foreigners and invested in the national economy. Private savings (Sp) is the difference between disposable income (income less taxes) and consumption (Sp = Y − T − C). Public savings (the negative of the fiscal budget deficit) is the difference between tax revenues and government spending (Sg = T − G). Foreign savings is the amount of extra imports the national economy can buy above the value of the exports sold abroad (Sf = M − X), which is approximately the negative of the current account balance.

Starting with the savings-investment equilibrium and then substituting and recombining the identities[2] yields an identity that highlights the relationship between the twin deficits but also reveals another key relationship, that between investment and private savings: (I − Sp) = Sg + Sf = (T − G) + (M − X). This accounting identity says that if private savings and

---

1. This is the familiar formula: Y = GDP = C + I + G + X − M.

2. Start with the savings-investment equality and substitute the identities: I = S = Sp + Sg + Sf = (Y − T − C) + (T − G) + (M − X).

Figure 2.2 Net private savings and investment, 1982-89

percentage of GDP

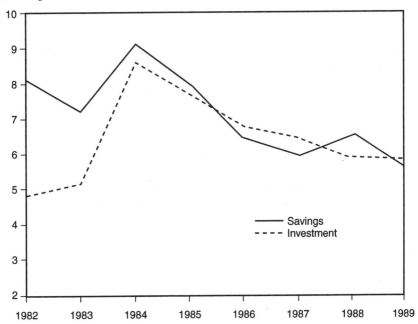

Sources: US Department of Commerce, *Survey of Current Business*; Council of Economic Advisers, *Economic Report of the President*.

domestic investment are about equal, or at least move by about the same amount, then the fiscal and external deficits would be twins—about the same size and moving in the same way. Indeed, from 1983 to 1989, private savings and investment did move together (figure 2.2).

Economic Reasoning Suggested That Common Forces Were Driving Both Deficits

In addition to the accounting identities, economic reasoning suggested that the deficits responded to the same economic fundamentals. During the 1980s, expansionary fiscal policy (as measured by the growing fiscal deficit) mixed with tight monetary policy to raise interest rates sharply and then keep them high. The high interest rates as well as a robust US economy encouraged international investment in US and dollar-denominated assets, and the exchange value of the dollar appreciated (figure 2.3). The appreciated dollar made US exports more expensive for foreigners to buy, and made imports cheaper. In addition, imports rose quickly as the US economy burst out of recession with a GDP growth rate of 7 percent.

Figure 2.3   Fiscal deficit, interest rate, and the dollar, 1980-98

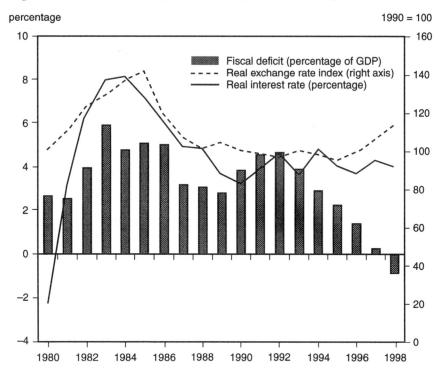

percentage   1990 = 100

Legend:
- Fiscal deficit (percentage of GDP)
- Real exchange rate index (right axis)
- Real interest rate (percentage)

Note: Real exchange rate is the nominal exchange rate adjusted by trade-weighted CPI inflation. Real interest rate is the 30-year Treasury bond rate adjusted for US inflation.

Sources: US Council of Economic Advisers, *Economic Report of the President;* US Department of Commerce, *International Transactions Tables;* IMF, *International Financial Statistics.*

Hence the external deficit grew larger on account of pressures originating from the appreciation of the dollar as well as from the robustness cf the expansion.[3] The deficits were thus twinned through the mechanism linking fiscal deficit to interest rates to exchange rate to external deficit.

This chain of causality could have unwound the same way—a smaller fiscal deficit reduces upward pressure on interest rates, the demand for dollar-denominated assets falls, the dollar depreciates, and the external deficit narrows—and indeed, it appeared that this logic held for a number of years in the late 1980s and early 1990s (see figure 2.3). But as the 1990s unfolded, this apparent chain of causality broke; the fiscal deficit shrank, but interest rates and particularly the exchange value of the dollar did not come down as far.

---

3. The role of income growth and that of changes in relative prices, including through changes in the exchange value of the dollar, are further discussed in chapter 8.

What Happened to Separate the Twins?

There are several answers to the question of what happened to the twins. One is that they were not really twins. In particular, from the perspective of the NIPA identities there were key changes in the behavior of private savings and investment in the 1990s, engendered in part by changes in monetary policy at home and abroad. A second answer is that the critical links between the fiscal deficit, interest rates, and the exchange value of the dollar were less tight than was generally thought. Finally, to take a somewhat different perspective on the puzzle, the dynamics of the US external balance depend importantly on the relative rates of growth of the United States and its trading partners; while the United States has grown rapidly since the mid-1990s, our trading partners generally have not.

In the 1990s, Investment Rates Grew Continuously, But Household Savings Collapsed; Foreign Savings Had to Fill the Gap

A first observation is that the relationship between the two deficits that is graphically discernible in the 1980s is less obvious when the figures are plotted over a longer time frame (figure 2.4). Long periods of current account surpluses coincided with moderate budget deficits in the 1950s and 1960s, and the very large fiscal deficits in the 1970s coincided with only negligible current account deficits. In this light, the twin deficits of the 1980s appear more an aberration than a common occurrence.

From a substantive viewpoint, the two deficits separated in part because private savings and business investment did not move together in the 1990s as they had in the 1980s, and in part because private savings and public savings moved in opposite directions. In the NIPA framework, the external deficit equals *national savings* (public plus private) minus investment. In the 1990s, although the fiscal deficit contracted (which means that public savings was rising), private savings was drifting downward. In addition, the savings rate for households, which is one component of private savings, declined dramatically (figure 2.5).[4]

---

4. The official household savings rate is a residual calculation from the NIPA definitions: personal disposable income minus personal consumption outlays. Its relationship to the economic concept of savings is questionable, and its trend behavior over time has become quite controversial, particularly as the measured rate fell below zero in early 1999. Gale and Sabelhaus (1999) show that if the NIPA definition is adjusted for other forms of retirement saving (such as federal and state retirement plans), the decline in the household savings rate is somewhat less dramatic, and the level remains above zero. By including consumer durables in household savings as well as adjusting for inflation and certain taxes, the rate of decline levels out even more. Finally, including capital gains makes a huge difference; indeed, it reverses the measured decline and, by this measure, the household savings rate in the highest in the past 40 years! However, the capital gains component is highly volatile.

Figure 2.4 The "twin deficits": A longer perspective

percentage of GDP

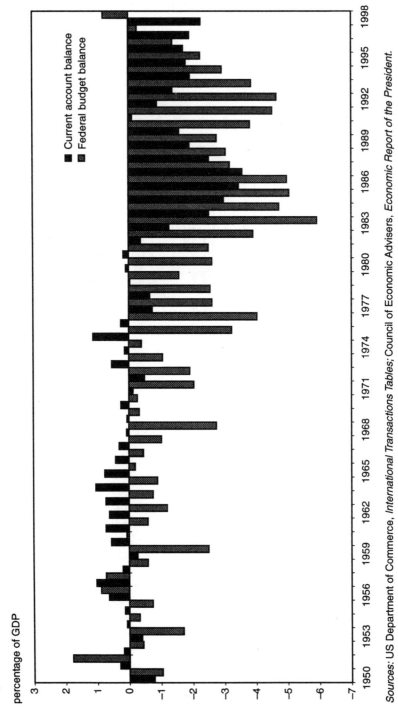

Sources: US Department of Commerce, *International Transactions Tables;* Council of Economic Advisers, *Economic Report of the President.*

Figure 2.5 US investment and savings by sector, 1980-98

percentage of GDP

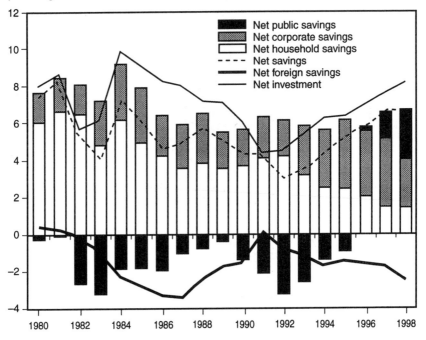

Source: US Department of Commerce, *Survey of Current Business.*

When the economy emerged from the 1981-82 recession, the rate of business investment shot up, as did the rate of private savings. Soon after, however, starting in 1984 and continuing through the 1991 recession, national savings and investment rates slowed. Even though the fiscal deficit improved as the recession ended, private savings rates declined. The gap between national savings and investment was filled by foreign savings.

After the 1991 recession, the disparity among the three components of national savings increased. The corporate savings rate (loosely speaking, profits) rose smartly. The fiscal deficit narrowed substantially as growth resumed and continued robustly. Throughout the 1980s and 1990s, however, the household savings rate generally continued to decline, and indeed it collapsed at the end of 1998.

These changes in the composition of national savings might matter for the evolution of the external deficit. Input-output accounts for the United States suggest that the import intensity of government output is about 17 percent, whereas the import intensity of consumer spending on goods is about 58 percent, and the import intensity of investment spending on goods is about 50 percent. Moreover, in contrast to the 1980s expansion, in which investment rates generally fell, economic activity in the 1990s has been powered by a continuous rise, to nearly a 17 percent rate, in real net investment for producers' durable equipment. Consequently, an increase in public savings that is matched by a fall in private savings would not wash out in the external accounts but would appear to favor imports. Overall, the sum of private and public savings has been insufficient by about 1 percent to finance all the desired private investment.

Finally, there is a statistical discrepancy of an additional 1 percent of GDP in the accounting for spending and saving in the US economy (see the addendum to this chapter for more details). Hence foreign savings of about 2 percent of GDP have been flowing into the United States to support private business investment and overall spending in the US economy.

Why has business investment increased as a share of GDP but household savings dropped so dramatically? A factor common to both is the dramatic increase in the value of corporations' equity, which comes from the continued robust growth of the US economy, the low rate of inflation, and the attractiveness to domestic and foreign savers alike of the US stock markets. The US savers who hold the highest fraction of their wealth in portfolio investments have tended to save a smaller fraction of their income as the value of their wealth rises. The unprecedented rise in the US stock market has tended to make investors more confident of the future value of their wealth, inducing them to reduce the portion of their income that they save (figure 2.6). At the same time, the climate of robust consumption and low inflation has encouraged business investment, so the savings-investment imbalance has widened.

An Increased Demand for Dollar Investments and High US Growth Rates Helped to Increase the External Deficit

The strength of the US economy has attracted foreign investment and has increased the use of the dollar as a vehicle for making those investments. Hence as the fiscal deficit contracted (reducing upward pressure on interest rates), the dollar exchange rate initially depreciated but then appreciated. The continued foreign demand for US financial assets unlinked the "twins" by breaking down the chain of logic that connected the fiscal deficit, interest rates, the exchange value of the dollar, and the external balance.

Initially, as the fiscal deficit narrowed, interest rates did come down and the exchange value of the dollar depreciated (see figure 2.3). However, into the 1990s the rapid increase in US stock market valuation attracted foreign investors, who helped bid up the markets as well as the value of the dollar (figure 2.7). In addition, the dollar solidified its position as the lead currency of issuance in the market for international debt securities (table 2.1). Hence the assumption that the reduction of the fiscal deficit would reduce interest rates, help to depreciate the dollar, and thus

Figure 2.6 Wealth and savings, 1970-98

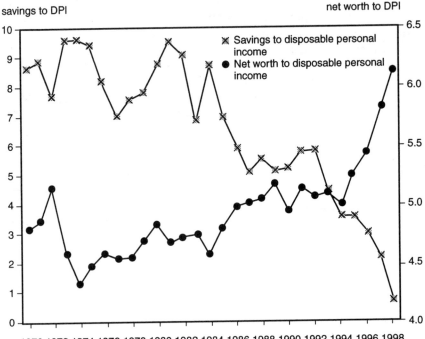

savings to DPI

net worth to DPI

DPI = disposable personal income
Note: Wealth or net worth refers to assets minus liabilities of households and nonprofit organizations.

Sources: Board of Governors of the Federal Reserve System, *Flow of Funds Accounts of the US; Federal Reserve Bulletin;* US Department of Commerce, *Survey of Current Business.*

close the external deficit was not borne out. In sum, the explanation that the external deficit widened because of rising domestic investment and falling private savings is consistent with this explanation based on the flows of foreign capital.

These approaches to analyzing the links between the fiscal and external deficits based on the domestic focus of the NIPA framework and on the financial focus of international capital flows do not adequately emphasize the key foreign ingredient in the determination of external balance: the difference between GDP growth here and abroad. This issue is addressed in more depth in chapter 8, but to state it briefly here, the magnitude of the external deficit depends in part on how strong is US demand for imports relative to foreign demand for US exports. When US economic ac-

Figure 2.7 Stock prices and foreign capital inflows, 1993-99 (1Q)

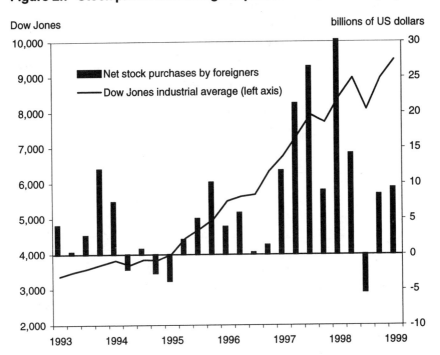

Source: US Department of Commerce, *International Transactions Tables*.

tivity is more robust than that of its trading partners, US import growth exceeds US export growth. As noted earlier, in the 1990s US economic activity generally has been more rapid than that of its major industrial-country trading partners, and has been spurred mostly by domestic demand (investment and consumption). Activity abroad generally has been slower and has been powered more by exports and less by domestic demand. In sum, the explanation that the US external deficit is caused by the *level and composition* of spending and savings *here* is consistent with the explanation that the external deficit is a consequence of the *difference* between GDP growth *here and abroad*.

Conclusion

Summary

■ The fiscal deficit and the external deficit looked like twins in the 1980s, and their linkage was supported by accounting identities as well as by

Table 2.1 Outstanding amounts and net issues of international debt securities, 1993-98 (percentage of total)

Currency	Amounts outstanding						Net issues					
	1993	1994	1995	1996	1997	1998	1993	1994	1995	1996	1997	1998
US dollar	41.0	37.3	35.1	39.1	44.3	44.9	15.9	25.7	23.8	48.4	56.5	57.5
Japanese yen	13.4	16.9	17.7	15.2	13.0	11.5	17.1	37.4	34.8	15.7	5.8	-4.3
EMU currencies	18.9	21.2	23.0	23.3	21.8	22.5	45.7	30.7	28.0	29.0	30.0	21.5
Total value (billions of US dollars)	2,038	2,442	2,803	3,154	3,542	4,234	198	285	312	543	596	592

EMU = European Monetary Union

Sources: IMF, *International Capital Markets* (September 1998); Bank for International Settlements, *International Banking and Financial Market Developments* (November 1998).

the logic of the economic chain running from fiscal deficit to higher interest rates to an appreciated dollar to a larger external deficit.

■ However, in the 1990s the two deficits began to decouple. First, as investment rates strengthened and the economy boomed, the fiscal deficit declined. The national savings rate did not rise, however, because the household savings rate declined. Foreign savings continued to fill the gap. One causal factor common to all these changes is the dramatic rise in the value of US stocks, which has spurred tax revenues and investment but which reduces the tendency of households to save.

■ In addition, the strength of the US economy has attracted foreign investment. The chain of causality from fiscal deficit to interest rates to exchange value of the dollar to external balance did not unwind in the 1990s as expected, in part because the robust US economy attracted substantial foreign inflows, which kept interest rates low but raised the dollar exchange rate.

■ Finally, the external deficit continues to grow because the US economy is growing faster and consumers are demanding more imported products than is the case for its trading partners.

■ Hence the explanations for the disappearance of the "twin deficits" relationship based on NIPA identities, on the economic logic of rate of return and financial flows, and on external balance and relative growth rates are all consistent.

Policy Discussion

■ Fiscal discipline has been a key underpinning of the economic success of the 1990s, and the unraveling of that discipline could imperil it. The policy challenge right now, however, is the downward trend in the household savings rate. The dramatic fall in the savings rate in the past year is a reflection of a strong economy and a robust stock market. But for the longer term, households are at risk of an imbalance between debt burdens and expected future earnings. It is dangerous to assume that the capital gains enjoyed over the past few years will continue indefinitely.

■ Raising the household savings rate has long been both a policy issue and a policy challenge. We should use this period of economic bounty to explore new ideas to ensure the sustainability of US consumption and economic growth. Clearly, households do respond to higher expected returns—witness the surge into the stock market as major indexes appear to move ever upward. Consequently, a reexamination of the disincentives to save current income in more stable investment vehicles is in order. Also, we should be careful to account properly for the savings that individuals do undertake.

Addendum: The NIPA Statistical Discrepancy

Most macroeconomic stories are best analyzed using the perspective of economic relationships over history, and the story of what happened to the "twin deficits" is based on an analysis of data over time. But looking at a snapshot of the data can also reveal information that may contribute to an understanding of the trends that are used to assess macroeconomic relationships.

An example relevant to the present case can be found in the relationship between the current account and the national savings-investment imbalance at the end of 1998. On the basis of national income and product accounts data, the difference between national savings and investment as a share of GDP is about 1 percent. Hence the current account deficit should be about 1 percent of GDP. But, as calculated from trade and investment data, the current account deficit is a bit more than 2 percent of GDP. The so-called statistical discrepancy makes up the 1 percentage point difference between these two measures.[5]

The statistical discrepancy in this case is the difference between gross domestic *product*—GDP—which is the value of production by labor and property in the United States, and gross domestic *income*—GDI—which is the value of the costs incurred and income accrued to the inputs that pro-

---

5. There is also a statistical discrepancy for external accounts between the current account balance and the recorded capital flows, which is discussed in chapter 9. Chapter 7 addresses alternative ways of measuring the current account deficit.

Figure 2.8 Statistical discrepancy between GDP and GDI, 1970-98

billions of US dollars

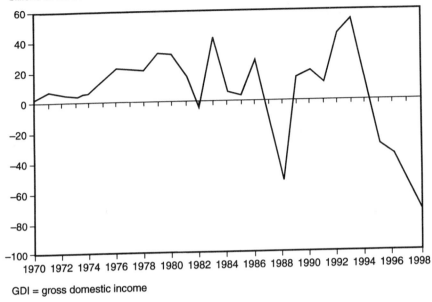

GDI = gross domestic income

Source: US Department of Commerce, *Survey of Current Business.*

duce the output. These two values should be the same. However, the two measures of the total economy come from very different source data, and so the two have differed, sometimes by large amounts (figure 2.8).

The difference between GDP and GDI may be related to high-technology products and activities. For example, the treatment of computer software differs between the two concepts. In the calculation of GDI, which is based in part on business tax returns, a software company is treated as a final producer that earns income and increases GDI. In GDP calculations, software purchases are considered an intermediate input and hence are included only implicitly in the value of final products. In addition, certain new business services, such as Internet access and cellular telephone services, which generate business taxes and income and thus augment GDI, are not yet included in consumption surveys and hence are not included in GDP calculations (see *Survey of Current Business,* August 1999, p. 19).

How the statistical discrepancy might be allocated to consumption and investment affects the macroeconomic identities, particularly the savings-investment balance. (Of course, if we knew how to allocate it, it would not be a statistical discrepancy.) If the bulk of the statistical discrepancy represents additional consumption (e.g., cell phones and unrecorded service-sector transactions), proper accounting would reduce net national savings. On the other hand, if software should be counted as a final investment product and not netted out as an intermediate input, the share of investment in GDP would be rising even faster than estimated. Either way, incorporating the statistical discrepancy into the macroeconomic identities helps to make the identities hold arithmetically at a point in time. Deciding how to allocate the statistical discrepancy could alter the underlying economic stories told in using data over time.

3

Has US Comparative Advantage Changed? Does This Affect Sustainability?

The evidence is overwhelmingly persuasive that the massive increase in world competition—a consequence of broadening trade flows—has fostered markedly higher standards of living . . . this surge in competitive trade has clearly owed, in large part, to significant advances in technological innovation.

—Alan Greenspan, chairman of the Federal Reserve Board,
"Technology and Trade," remarks before the Dallas Ambassadors Forum,
Dallas, Texas (16 April 1999)

[T]he globalization system . . . is not static, but a dynamic ongoing process: globalization involves the inexorable integration of markets, nation-states and technologies to a degree never witnessed before—in a way that is enabling individuals, corporations and nation-states to reach around the world farther, faster, deeper and cheaper than ever before. . . .

—Thomas L. Friedman, *The Lexus and the Olive Tree* (1999)

Why Trade?

People trade because they want different things, have different skills, and earn different amounts of money. With individuals represented by their national aggregates, countries trade for the same reasons. Countries differ from one another in terms of resources and the techniques firms use to produce goods and services. People value goods and services differently, depending on their income and tastes. Investors in financial assets have different preferences for risk, return, and diversification. These differences are reflected across countries as differences in costs of production, prices for products and services, and rates of return on and "exposures"[1] to financial assets.

Because costs, prices, and returns differ across countries, it makes sense for a country to trade some of what it produces most cheaply and holds less dear to people who want it more and for whom production is costly or even impossible. While this may be most obvious in the case of goods, the concept holds as well for services and financial assets, and is applicable to rich and poor, large and small countries alike.

This concept is known as "comparative advantage." The goods and services that are *relatively* cheaper to produce and have the *relatively* lower price, or financial assets that have a *relatively* more advantageous risk-return profile, are those in which a country has comparative advantage. The country will export these to obtain other products and assets that are different and more desired.

Where Does Comparative Advantage Come From?

Comparative advantage motivates people to trade. Because comparative advantage comes from differences in *relative prices*, it means that characteristics of both supply and demand matter. Thus comparative advantage for a country results from a complex combination of the characteristics that are difficult to change (such as natural resource endowments), characteristics of the overall country that change relatively slowly (such as the share of production and consumption of services relative to the share of manufacturing, agriculture, and mining), characteristics of production technology that in some cases can change relatively quickly (such as through turnkey production technology), and characteristics of individual preferences (such as for a particular kind or quality of products, services, or financial assets).

Some easy examples of comparative advantage come from trade in commodities, where resource endowments are quite important. For example, the United States imports coffee and tea because people want to drink these beverages, but the North American climate is not suitable for the plants that produce the beans and leaves. Similarly, the United States buys oil on international markets because it can import it at a price lower than the cost of extracting it from US oil wells—current production technology combined with resource endowments and the substantial US use

---

1. Financial "exposure" is a way of describing the characteristics of a financial asset held by an investor. Financial exposure incorporates country, firm, currency, maturity, volatility, and other characteristics.

Table 3.1 US government bonds in the global bond market, 1997

Global bond market, total outstanding (trillions of US dollars)	24.1
Government bond share (percentage)	59.6
Share of US government bonds in global bond market (percentage)	27.6
Share of Japanese government bonds (percentage)	11.7
Share of EMU government bonds (percentage)	14.7

EMU = European Monetary Union
Note: The EMU government bond percentage is the sum of government bonds issued by Germany, Italy, France, the Netherlands, Belgium, Spain, Austria, Finland, and Ireland.
Source: Merrill Lynch (1998).

of oil mean that the Middle East has a comparative advantage in oil production, so Middle Eastern nations export oil to the United States.

An example of comparative advantage in financial assets seems a bit more complicated, but the principle emerges nonetheless. The United States has a very mature market for government bonds. Any investor who wishes to hold risk-free and liquid assets at maturities ranging from 30 days to 30 years can buy US government assets. Because the market is so well developed, the United States has a comparative advantage in government-backed financial instruments and hence exports them to investors around the world (table 3.1).

"Two-Way" Trade in Similar Products Is the Largest Component of US Trade

A substantial amount of US trade consists of "two-way" trade (importing and exporting) of similar types of goods, services, and assets, ranging from autos to tourism to bonds. This trade is sometimes called intra-industry trade, because it was first analyzed for trade in goods. "Industry" is a bit of a misnomer now, since there is tremendous cross-border trade in services and assets as well as in goods.

While such two-way trade would seem to run counter to comparative advantage, in fact it confirms the principle. Why would a country import and export things that seem to be similar in use and are classified as such by the statistical agencies? A clear example is tourism, where the unique attributes of a country are the reason for the trade. To experience Rio or New York, you have to go there. Tourism creates a natural two-way trade flow as Brazilians visit New York and US citizens visit Rio.

Another example is in products that are similar in terms of how they are used—and therefore are classified in the same grouping by statistical agencies—but differ in quality or functionality. Polartec anoraks and polyester windbreakers are both jackets, but they satisfy different consumer tastes and pocketbooks in the United States and abroad. So the United States imports polyester windbreakers (which are cheaper to produce abroad) and exports Polartec anoraks (which are produced in the United States using special production inputs and techniques). Supercomputers and desktop models are both computers, but their functionality is different. Both types of computers are produced in the United States as well as abroad, with different specifications. Since some consumers and businesses in the United States and abroad need supercomputers and some need desktop models, the United States exports and imports both.

Trade in financial assets offers another example of two-way trade. Investors buy and sell assets to achieve a desired risk, return, and diversification profile for their portfolio of wealth. US investors buy financial assets issued by corporations and governments abroad in order to diversify their portfolio—to increase returns and/or to alter the volatility of returns compared to what they could obtain if they held a portfolio with only US assets. A diversified portfolio of financial assets allows the investor to achieve a more favorable risk-return frontier (a higher return for a given risk) compared to holding a portfolio that contains only domestic assets (figure 3.1).

A third kind of intra-industry trade comes from differences in consumer tastes combined with economies of scale in production technology. Intra-industry trade in automobiles offers a classic example. BMW, Jaguar, and Cadillac all produce expensive, high-performance automobiles. Because there are economies of scale in the production of a particular kind of car, it does not make sense to produce at home only a small run of a particular variety of car, just enough to satisfy the domestic demand. Instead firms choose a production location where a large run of cars can be produced and transported most cheaply to their final destination and then trade cars across borders to satisfy demand abroad. Hence automobile imports and exports satisfy the full range of tastes for different kinds of cars in the populations of the United States and of other countries.

As countries become more similar in terms of the resources they have and the production technologies they employ, differences in tastes become the driving force behind trade flows. Table 3.2 illustrates that an index of two-way trade in goods of similar use but different characteristics is greatest for high-income areas that are broadly similar to the United States—such as Canada and Europe. The index for two-way trade with countries with different resources and with per capita incomes substantially below that of the United States, such as China and India, is generally low.

What Do We Trade and How Has It Changed over Time?

The broadest decomposition of US trade is into the categories of goods (often called merchandise), services, and financial assets. Of course, bal-

Figure 3.1 Risk, return, and the efficient international diversified portfolio

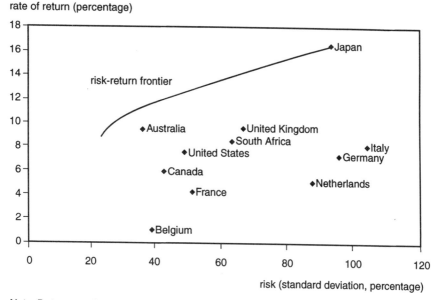

rate of return (percentage)

Note: Data are estimated, 1959-66.

Source: Grubel (1968).

ance of payments convention puts goods and services on one side of the ledger and financial assets on the other. Breaking each of these categories down further, as illustrated in table 3.3, helps in analyzing what the United States trades, how that has changed over time, and how trade is related to the domestic economy.

For goods, one useful classification is "end-use."[2] This grouping reflects stage of processing (e.g., autos vs. industrial supplies) and ultimate buyer (capital goods—generally purchased by businesses—versus consumer goods—generally purchased by households). The end-use classification can be matched up to the broad categories of consumption and investment in the national income and product accounts.

Among services, a helpful decomposition distinguishes between "locomotive" services (e.g., travel, passenger fares, or other transportation);

---

2. Other groupings include the Standard Industrial Classification (SIC), which was replaced by the North American Industry Classification System (AICS) in 1997, and the Standard International Trade Classification (SITC), which was replaced by the Harmonized System (HS) in 1995. Each highlights a particular feature of the good or service. Depending on the question, one or another of the statistical disaggregations could be best, but none is perfect for all questions. A key difficulty is that the disaggregation schemes commonly used for domestic data match up rather poorly with data on internationally traded goods and services.

Table 3.2 Index of two-way trade in selected product categories

Item	High income	Middle income	Low income
Crude materials, inedible, except fuels	85	63	36
Petroleum, petroleum products, and related materials	29	28	7
Chemicals and related products, n.e.s.	98	34	76
Medicinal and pharmaceutical products	98	24	72
Textile yarn, fabrics, made-up articles, related products	97	94	34
Power generating machinery and equipment	88	82	36
General industrial machinery and equipment	83	64	39
Electrical machinery, apparatuses, and appliances	99	96	88
Travel goods, handbags, and similar containers	56	7	2
Articles of apparel and clothing accessories	75	36	3
Footwear	29	4	1

n.e.s. = not elsewhere specified

Note: Index = {(X − M) − IX − MI} / (X + M) * 100.

Source: Statistics Canada, World Trade Analyzer 1997.

"other private" services (e.g., education, financial services, and business and professional services); service flows based on intellectual property (e.g., royalties and license fees); and service flows between governments (e.g., military services).

Finally, in the category of financial flows, a common disaggregation is based on who issued the obligation (official versus private entity), what is the extent of ownership and control (direct investment vs. portfolio investment), and within portfolio investment, whether or not the obligation has a fixed principal value (bond vs. equity). These distinctions are useful when considering how economic data and policies affect investor behavior and thus affect trade in financial assets.

Since 1975 the composition of US exports and imports—and particularly the latter—has become more concentrated in particular sectors, yet at the same time more trade is two-way trade. In exports, the share of services has increased, with "locomotive" services and "other private" services predominating. The comparative advantage enjoyed by the United States in the service-sector industries is reflected not only in their rising share in total exports but also in the positive and increasing net export balance in services (figure 3.2). Among goods, capital goods in particular have risen in share of total exports, and both capital and consumer goods have increased dramatically in share of total imports. The extent of two-way trade in capital goods and consumer goods is quite different, however, and may have important implications for the sustainability of the

Table 3.3 Composition of US trade in goods, services, and financial accounts (nominal, percentage of total)

	1975	1997
Exports	100.0	100.0
Goods	80.8	72.5
Foods, feeds, and beverages	14.4	5.5
Industrial supplies and materials	22.5	16.9
Capital goods, except autos	27.4	31.4
Automotive vehicles, engines, and parts	7.6	7.8
Consumer goods, except autos	4.9	8.3
Other	4.8	2.6
Services	19.2	27.5
Travel and passenger fares	4.3	10.0
Other transportation	4.4	2.9
Other private	2.2	9.0
Royalties and license fees	3.2	3.6
Military and government	5.1	2.0
Capital outflow	100.0	100.0
Government assets	10.9	0.2
Private assets	89.1	99.8
Direct investment	35.9	25.5
Foreign securities	15.7	18.4
Foreign stocks	n.a.	8.6
Foreign bonds	n.a.	9.8
Other claims (includes banks)	37.5	56.0
Imports	100.0	100.0
Goods	81.7	83.7
Foods, feeds, and beverages	8.0	3.8
Industrial supplies and materials	40.9	20.7
Capital goods, except autos	8.5	24.3
Automotive vehicles, engines, and parts	9.7	13.4
Consumer goods, except autos	11.0	18.4
Other	2.3	2.8
Services	18.3	16.3
Travel and passenger fares	7.2	6.6
Other transportation	4.7	2.8
Other private	1.3	4.6
Royalties and licence fees	0.4	0.9
Military and government	4.6	1.4
Capital inflow	100.0	100.0
Foreign official assets	40.9	2.2
Other assets	59.1	97.8
Direct investment	15.2	12.7
US Treasury securities and currency	23.8	23.4
Other securities	14.6	26.8
Stocks	n.a.	9.0
Bonds	n.a.	17.8
Other liabilities (includes banks)	5.5	34.9

Sources: US Department of Commerce, *Survey of Current Business; International Transactions Tables.*

Figure 3.2 US balance on goods and services, 1970-99 (1Q)

billions of US dollars

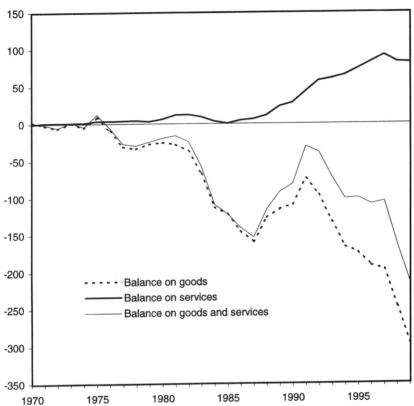

Note: Figures for 1999 are based on first-quarter data.

Sources: Bureau of Economic Analysis, *International Transactions Tables,* Historical Data; US Department of Commerce, *Survey of Current Business.*

current account deficit (figure 3.3). A zero balance of trade within a category (when averaged over the business cycle) implies a high degree of two-way trade. Two-way trade measured over all trading partners is lowest for consumer goods and autos.[3]

---

3. If the overall trade balance is in deficit, then some sectors will have to be in deficit as well. However, if the extent of two-way trade is equal across all sectors, then all would be in deficit to some degree—more explicitly in deficit in proportion to the size of the sector in overall trade. The inference about the degree of two-way trade in the end-use categories of US trade comes from the persistence and trend behavior of the consumer goods and auto sectors.

Figure 3.3 Balance on goods, by sector: Evidence of two-way trade

billions of US dollars

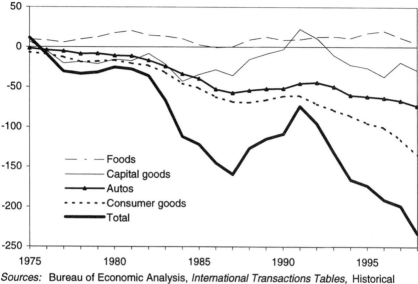

Sources: Bureau of Economic Analysis, *International Transactions Tables,* Historical Diskette; US Department of Commerce, *Survey of Current Business.*

Rising Services Trade and Implications for Sustainability

The rising importance of exports of services reflects the ongoing shift in the US economy toward a service-sector base. In the past 20 years the share of the service sector in US GDP increased from about 60 percent to 72 percent. The demand for high-quality services at home contributes to a global comparative advantage in the delivery of many different professional services.

Studies by McKinsey Global Institute (1992) of selected service-sector industries suggest that labor productivity in the United States in these sectors exceeds that of its major competitors (Germany, France, United Kingdom, and Japan) by perhaps 30 percent in airlines, 30 to 40 percent in retail banking, and 20 to 50 percent in telecommunications. In part because the domestic market is so well developed, the United States is also the world's leading exporter of business and professional services.

Properly accounting for service-sector transactions is difficult enough in the domestic economy, but it is even more challenging when services cross borders. One type of business that is important in both the US domestic economy and international trade but is increasingly difficult to value properly is packaged computer software (see OECD 1998; see also

Table 3.4 US exports of software: Alternative measures

	Firms' sales	US BOP data	
US global exports, 1995 (billions of US dollars)	13	3	

	US BOP data	OECD data	Japanese survey data
US exports to Japan, 1994 (millions of US dollars)	260	–	–
Japanese imports from the United States, 1994 (millions of US dollars)	–	210	2,400

BOP = balance of payments

Source: OECD (1998a, 11-13).

the discussion in the addendum to chapter 2). Valuing trade transactions in computer software is particularly challenging because different countries account for them in different ways and because there are so many modes of delivery. For example, packaged software can be recorded as an export on a CD-ROM in a box or loaded on a computer; through license fees for printing via a "gold master" disc; via affiliate sales, in which profits accrue in investment income; and, finally, via Internet digital delivery. It is safe to say that no national statistical system is sophisticated enough or flexible enough to handle this range of modes of delivery.

How important is this industry that is so hard to track? The Organization for Economic Cooperation and Development (OECD), using firms' sales data, estimates that the total value of software sales by leading US vendors was $29 billion in 1995, of which sales outside the United States amounted to $13 billion (table 3.4). Thus sales are large and increasing, and the share of exports is nearly 50 percent. Yet data in the US balance of payments statistics report software exports of just $3 billion (OECD 1998, 13 [table 7]).

Bilateral data are no better. US balance of payments data on exports of software media (e.g., diskettes, CD-ROMs) to Japan differ from the corresponding OECD data on Japan's imports from the United States by 20 percent ($260 million vs. $210 million). Moreover, a survey from Japan estimated the value of software products imported from the United States at $2.4 billion, an order of magnitude larger than the OECD data.[4]

The share of services in US exports should increase further as our trading partners grow, mature, and demand more services. In general, the service sector as a share of GDP is lower in middle- and lower-income countries than it is in the high-income countries, and the share of services in US

---

4. The statistical agencies are working to improve the data, in cooperation with their counterparts in other countries, and addressing ways to improve coverage of small-value exports and services. How to deal appropriately with computer software and other such products presents a particularly vexing, but critical, challenge.

Table 3.5 Role of services, 1995 (percentage)

	Service share of GDP	Service share of US exports to the country/region
World	49.6[a]	22.0
Europe	69.1[b]	34.6
South and Central America	56.6	25.4
South Korea and Singapore	57.5	18.6
China and India	36.6	18.1[c]

a. Average of 129 countries where data are available.
b. Average of Austria, France, Netherlands, and Norway, because of limited availability of data.
c. China only.

Sources: World Bank, World Development Indicators; US Department of Commerce, Survey of Current Business (October 1998); International Transactions Tables; US International Sales and Purchases of Private Services.

exports to these countries tends to be lower than the average share for services in total exports (table 3.5). In addition, liberalization of the service sector (even in the upper-income countries) has just begun, with the adoption of the General Agreement on Trade in Services (GATS) in the Uruguay Round of the General Agreement on Tariffs and Trade. The proper protection and accounting for intellectual property such as computer software was also addressed in the Uruguay Round.[5] While two-way trade in services will also increase, maintaining a US comparative advantage in services and opening markets abroad will help to ensure that net trade in services contributes positively to the overall US trade balance.

Globalization of Production Is Essential for Comparative Advantage in Some Products

A key feature of US trade is the decomposing of the production process into separable functions that can then be allocated around the world to countries that possess comparative advantage in that particular phase of the production process. The pieces are then brought together for final assembly and sale.

Such globalization of production is particularly prevalent in computers and related products; the two-way trade measure in this industry is quite high (figure 3.4). Semiconductors, computers, and parts and accessories,

---

5. For more on the GATS agreement and the Uruguay Round, see Schott (1994, 1996).

Figure 3.4 Semiconductors, computers, and peripherals in US trade, 1980-96

A. Exports

billions of US dollars

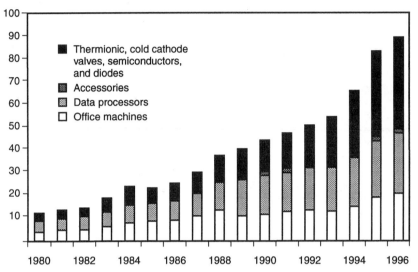

B. Imports

billions of US dollars

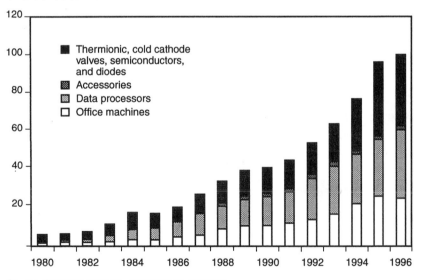

Source: Statistics Canada, World Trade Analyzer.

which are classified as capital goods, are fast-growing segments of both exports and imports. These categories combined now account for about 40 percent of trade in capital goods (30 percent of exports and about 40 percent of imports). The rapid growth of this sector is a primary reason for the large and increasing share of capital goods in both US exports and imports. Why is there so much exporting and importing in this category of goods?

The extent of two-way trade reflects the advantages that accrue to producers when they decompose production into stages of processing that are distributed to the most advantageous locations worldwide. The United States has the comparative advantage in producing and exporting certain parts of the production process (the high-value-added processor chips, the innovative and complex software, and the fully assembled product), but has relinquished parts of the production process to other countries where that stage of processing can be completed more cheaply (memory chips, "canned" software, and most peripherals). The United States cannot have comparative advantage in the export of the final product if it cannot combine its own comparative advantage in the initial ingredients with the comparative advantage of other countries applied to the production process at critical stages. Comparative advantage thus can be a function of trade itself.

Two-Way Trade in Financial Assets Reveals US Comparative Advantage

The US current account has been in deficit for nearly 20 years. From an accounting standpoint, this means that the United States has been a borrower for this whole period. Does this mean that capital flows have run only in one direction, into the United States? Not at all. Throughout this period, there have been two-way flows of different kinds of financial assets. In recent years, even as the trade deficit has widened, the two-way flows have exploded, and gross flows are simply huge.

Figure 3.5 details the types of financial products and ownership relationships that characterize US trade in financial assets. Net US investment abroad (capital outflows) is above the zero line, and net foreign investment in the United States (capital inflows) by the rest of the world is below the line. While financial flows have always been two-way, the two directions of trade expand and contract together, broadly following the US and global business cycles. That is, when the US economy slows (as it did in 1982, 1990-91, and 1994) or foreign economies slow (as they did in 1997-98), net *cross-border* investment flows slow as well. This behavior is consistent with investment and financial flows *within* an economy over the business cycle.

Examining the detail of net capital flows reveals that there is substantial two-way trade in similar kinds of financial assets. For example, two-

Figure 3.5 Selected US and foreign financial transactions, 1975–99 (1Q)

billions of US dollars

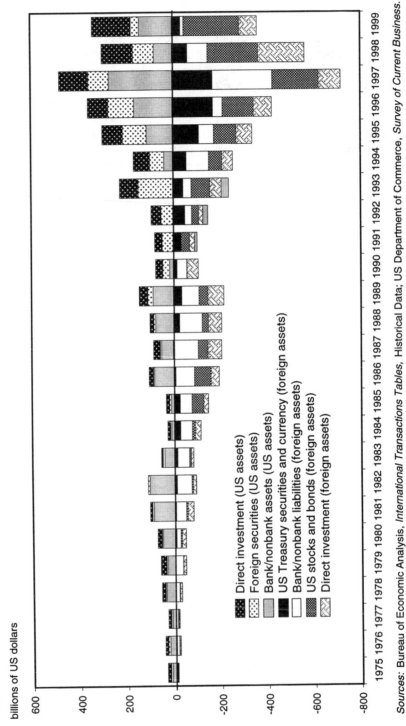

- Direct investment (US assets)
- Foreign securities (US assets)
- Bank/nonbank assets (US assets)
- US Treasury securities and currency (foreign assets)
- Bank/nonbank liabilities (foreign assets)
- US stocks and bonds (foreign assets)
- Direct investment (foreign assets)

Sources: Bureau of Economic Analysis, *International Transactions Tables,* Historical Data; US Department of Commerce, *Survey of Current Business.*

way flows through banks were particularly important through the mid-1980s, and were the principal form of capital flows. Such two-way flows can result when firms export to or move to a foreign market but continue to do their banking business with a firm at home. In this case, two-way flows of goods can contribute to two-way flows of bank finance.

More recently, the internationalization and liberalization of financial markets and growing wealth in the United States and abroad have fueled huge increases in cross-border investment in stocks and bonds. But the portfolio compositions of US and foreign investors are somewhat different. US net investment (capital outflows) into private foreign assets are a bit overweighted toward bank/nonbank flows, with private securities and direct investment each a significant share of the set of investments. US investors hold virtually no foreign government securities. In contrast, foreign investors in US assets hold a portfolio heavily weighted toward US government securities. In recent years, about one-third of net financial flows have been into these securities. Private bank/nonbank and securities flows have also been important, and direct investment was particularly large in 1998.

That US government securities have an international comparative advantage among financial assets appears clear. But this comparative advantage could come from the greater availability of these assets (as noted in table 3.1) or from a greater desire on the part of the foreign investor to hold high-yielding, nearly risk-free assets that they apparently cannot obtain from any source other than the US government.

In the future, if the US fiscal balance remains near zero, fewer government bonds will be available for investors. If the preference remains strong abroad for this type of asset, then foreign demand for US government securities will help sustain the current account deficit. In addition, the strong demand with reduced supply could reduce US government borrowing rates. On the other hand, should the market for US government securities dry up (say, if the publicly held component of the national debt were retired using federal budget surpluses), then foreigners might be less willing to buy US government securities. Once again, comparative advantage is not exogenous but is the outcome of complex interaction among economic forces and actors.

Conclusion

Summary

- Countries trade because differences in resources, technologies, and tastes lead to differences in costs, prices, and rates of return. Consumers, producers, and investors benefit from these differences when they trade goods, services, and financial assets.

- In trade between countries that have similar resources and income levels, typically there is substantial two-way trade in what might appear to be similar products but which satisfy tastes that are not identical.

- The composition of US trade reflects changing tastes and comparative advantage at home and abroad as well as the global integration of production and distribution. The example of computers shows that the success and growth of the US computer industry depends on combining US comparative advantage in both the initial and the final stages with comparative advantage abroad in intermediate stages of production.

- The desire to diversify financial portfolios as well as the desire to globalize the production and distribution of goods and services has led to a remarkable rise in the two-way flows of financial assets. Only in the case of US government securities do there appear to be few comparable assets abroad.

Policy Discussion

- Policies that limit trade restrict the benefits that come from cost, price, and variety. Equally important, restrictions on moving part of the production process abroad or limiting certain imports can undermine exports and may hurt the creation of comparative advantage for new final goods.

- The US service sector has global comparative advantage. As our trading partners develop and grow, their demand for services will rise. Ensuring open markets for competitive US exporters will raise US export levels and will benefit the recipients. A comparative advantage in services and a growing service-sector trade surplus would help sustain the overall trade deficit. Service-sector trade negotiations should be a priority.

- Foreign demand for US government securities has been an important source of financing of the US external deficit. The maturity and liquidity of the US government securities market has no equal in the world now. But will this strong demand continue as the Japanese government securities market develops and as government bonds in Europe are increasingly issued in euro, or will competition ensue? If the strong demand continues even as the US budget position stays in surplus, the value of the US instruments should rise. On the other hand, if both US and foreign investors increasingly see foreign government instruments as substitutes for US government securities, we should see increasing two-way trade in government securities. Moreover, if the federal budget surplus is used to retire the national debt, the market for US government securities would no longer be so liquid.

II

How Does Increasing Integration into the Global Economy Affect Sustainability?

4

How Does Trade Affect the American Worker?

[A]n increase in U.S. trade deficits will eliminate relatively more high-wage jobs, especially for workers with less than a college education. . . . [A]verage incomes will decline . . . as trade deficits grow.

—Robert E. Scott and Jesse Rothstein, "American Jobs and the Asian Crisis: The Employment Impact of the Coming Rise in the U.S. Trade Deficit," Briefing Paper, Economic Policy Institute (January 1998)

Trade deficits do not cost jobs. In fact, rising trade deficits correlate with falling unemployment rates. . . . If the trade deficit really is one of our nation's most pressing problems, the surest and swiftest way to tackle it would be to engineer a deep recession.

—Daniel T. Griswold, "America's Maligned and Misunderstood Trade Deficit," Center for Trade Policy Studies, Cato Institute (24 April 1998)

Policy discussions at all levels as well as academic research have been marked by a good deal of rhetoric on the relationship between the globalization of the US economy and the dynamics of the US labor market. Imports and the growing trade deficit have been cited as important (or even principal) causes of the loss of manufacturing jobs, the increase in income inequality, and the stagnation in real wages. Policy discussions and research alike have sometimes confounded two factors that affect the relationship between globalization and the labor market. The first is how changes in the *trade balance* affect the labor market, and the second is how changes in *export and import flows*, the components of the trade balance, affect the labor market.

A close look at the trade balance reveals its macroeconomic underpinnings: Trade deficits are driven by expenditure greater than production at home and by faster growth at home than abroad. Contrary to the rhetoric, the trade deficit widens when US growth is good and job opportunities abound, and it shrinks when an economic slowdown occurs and the unemployment rate rises. Thus the relationship between the trade balance and overall conditions in the labor market is quite clear.

The more complex relationship is in how trade flows, and particularly the changing levels and composition of trade, affect workers. Some research does suggest that imports have contributed to wage inequality in the United States, but these conclusions could be significantly biased by the exclusion of exports from these analyses. More important, less research considers how relative wages are affected by technology as well as by trade.

Indeed, empirical investigations that try to explain labor market conditions in the United States principally by using the forces of trade cannot explain two general observations about how the US labor market has changed over the past two decades. First, although the relative wages of unskilled labor have fallen, rather than using more of this cheaper labor, firms in fact use less of it and instead employ more skilled labor. Second, a closer examination of the rising income or wage inequality (which is often measured as the relative wage of skilled vs. unskilled workers) reveals that it is the rise in wage inequality *within* an industrial sector and *among* apparently similar workers that accounts for a greater proportion of the overall rise in wage dispersion; it is not the increase in wage dispersion *across* industries and skills that is most important in driving the overall increase in wage inequality (see, for example, Burtless 1995). To be concrete, for example, there is greater variation in the wage rate among skilled workers in, say, the textile industry than there is between the wages of skilled workers in textiles and skilled workers in glassware. Technological change and the increased demand for skilled workers both at home and abroad help to explain these general observations about the US labor market.

Trade and technological change are related, however. Trade is an important force supporting or driving technological change. New analysis (discussed below) suggests that increasing demand for skills in both domestic and international marketplaces is driving up the wages of the relatively more skilled workers. Hence the policy focus should be on education and skill-training of workers to take advantage of job opportunities in the expanding sectors. Policies that restrict trade are a blunt instrument to help some workers and could slow technological change and thus hurt long-term US growth potential, which benefits everyone (see chapter 5).

The Trade Deficit and Labor Market Dynamics

From the perspective of the overall economy and the overall labor market, it is quite clear that a trade deficit does not cause recessions or unemploy-

Figure 4.1 Trade, recessions, and unemployment, 1970-98

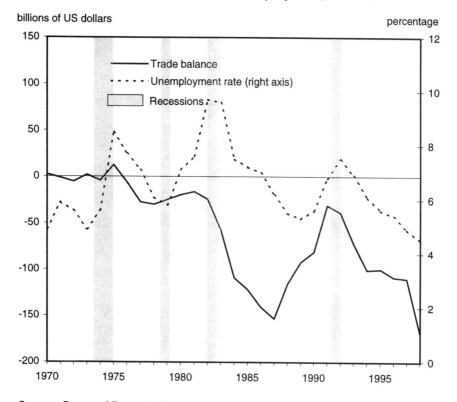

billions of US dollars

percentage

Sources: Bureau of Economic Analysis, International Transactions Tables; US Department of Labor, Employment Situation.

ment. This can be shown in several ways. For example, the relationships can be seen clearly in the correlation between the US trade balance, the unemployment rate, and periods of recession: As the economy slows, the unemployment rate rises, incomes fall, and the trade deficit narrows (figure 4.1).[1] This relationship between robust economic growth and a negative trade balance is not just a characteristic of the US economy, as the alternative presentation in figure 4.2 shows. Across the major industrial nations, trade balances that are positive on average are associated with GDP growth that is slow on average. Finally, employment creation and trade deficits tend to go together. The countries with the highest rate of increase in number of jobs also tend to be the countries with negative trade positions (figure 4.3).

In short, the data contradict the notion that a growing trade deficit costs jobs overall or slows the rate of growth of the economy overall. A more

1. Chapter 8 reviews in more detail the relationships between income and trade flows.

Figure 4.2 Economic growth and trade balances of G-7 countries, 1992-97

average annual GDP growth
(percentage)

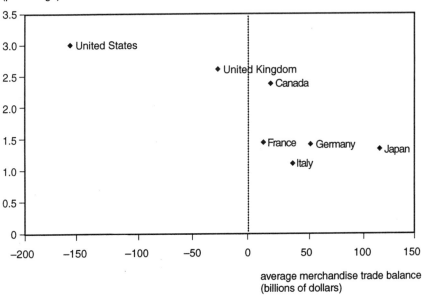

average merchandise trade balance
(billions of dollars)

Source: Organization for Economic Cooperation and Development, *OECD Economic Outlook* (December 1998).

interesting line of inquiry considers how the level and composition of exports and imports, the two components of the trade deficit, might change relative wages or the distribution of jobs among types of workers or across sectors.

Change over Time in US Exposure to Trade

At one time, the United States was considered a "closed" economy—that is, US GDP was little affected by international forces; whether exports or imports were rising or falling just did not much affect the economy. However, to find this state of affairs we have to go back to the 1950s, when the share of exports plus imports was less than 10 percent of GDP (figure 4.4). Starting about 30 years ago, the share of imports in GDP began a rapid, at times dramatic, rise. For exports, while the increase over the years in the share of GDP directly exposed to external demand has been nearly as great, the direction has not always been upward. Now, about one-fourth of GDP (nearly 30 percent in real terms) is directly influenced

Figure 4.3 Employment growth and trade balances of G-7 countries, 1992-97

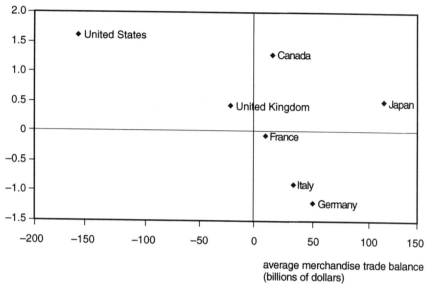

average annual employment growth
(percentage)

average merchandise trade balance
(billions of dollars)

Source: Organization for Economic Cooperation and Development, *OECD Economic Outlook* (December 1998).

by trade forces, split about equally between export exposure and import exposure.

This aggregate measure of global exposure masks differences in the pace of change in exposure of different sectors of the US economy to trade (table 4.1). In the production of goods, which represented about 20 percent of GDP in 1998, direct exposure to trade—that is, imports plus exports as a share of sector-specific GDP—is a remarkable 60 percent, nearly twice the exposure just 15 years ago. Moreover, the share of goods output affected by imports is 10 percentage points greater than the figure for exports. When disaggregated further into durable goods and nondurable goods, the total exposure of these subsectors is higher and the disparity between export and import exposure even greater.

On the other hand, the exposure of the service-producing sector to international trade is far less, and the increase over the past 20 years less dramatic. Although trade in services is growing faster than trade in goods (see chapter 3), the services component of GDP is growing even more rapidly; thus the direct exposure of the service sector to trade remains much lower, about 10 percent overall.

Figure 4.4 Exports and imports as share of GDP, 1929-98
(nominal dollar basis)

percentage of GDP

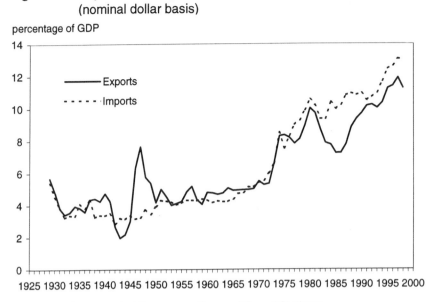

Source: US Department of Commerce, *Survey of Current Business.*

Using the standard global exposure measure in this simple decomposition into exports and imports of goods and services highlights two points. First, trade affects different groups of producers, workers, and consumers differently, as those involved with or purchasing products from the goods-producing sectors are affected much more by trade than those in the service-producing sectors. Second, the exposure through imports vs. exports is not the same. To the extent that exports and imports affect workers differently, the effect would be felt most in the goods-producing sector, where the imbalance between exports and imports is the greatest.

A Model of Global Exposure and Worker Wages

The theory of how changes in global exposure affect workers' wages is often analyzed in the Heckscher-Ohlin-Samuelson (HOS) framework. This standard trade model assumes that two economies that trade with each other have different types of labor (say, skilled labor in the United States and unskilled labor in another country), but identical tastes and technology. It is a static, long-run model that assumes full employment

Table 4.1 Export and import shares of GDP matched by sector (percentage)

	1975	1985	1990	1998
Real (chained 1992 dollars)				
Goods				
Exports	11.6	11.8	17.0	24.7
Imports	13.3	19.6	21.6	35.0
Services				
Exports	3.1	3.8	5.3	6.3
Imports	2.5	3.6	3.9	4.4
Nominal				
Goods				
Exports, total	15.3	13.3	18.1	21.9
Durable goods	22.7	19.0	28.0	34.4
Automotive vehicles	10.5	9.0	10.7	11.5
Nondurable goods	18.8	13.8	19.0	24.0
Imports, total	13.8	20.6	23.1	30.1
Durable goods	16.3	28.3	33.5	45.1
Automotive vehicles	12.2	14.7	15.3	17.5
Nondurable goods	21.1	36.1	46.1	50.0
Services				
Exports	3.6	3.9	5.3	6.0
Imports	3.2	3.6	4.0	3.8

Source: US Department of Commerce, *National Income and Product Accounts.*

and balanced trade, and therefore it cannot address issues of the trade *balance*, only trade *flows*.[2]

How do trade flows change relative wages and the distribution of jobs in this framework? The transmission mechanism is as follows: When trade opens up or increases between the United States (relatively well endowed with skilled labor) and the other country (relatively well endowed with unskilled labor), the result is a drop in the relative price of the good that is produced using relatively more of the unskilled labor. This drop in relative price causes an increase in US imports of that good. The rise in

---

2. The HOS model is widely used because of its elegance and simplicity. However, it does not explain very well trade patterns of industrialized countries, in part because much of this trade is "intra-industry" (between countries of similar factor endowments but different tastes). The HOS model does better at explaining North-South trade flows. Moreover, since it is a model of balanced trade, it is of little use when trade flows are not balanced—for example, when countries are at different points in their business cycles.

imports would tend to reduce the US demand for unskilled labor, but because full employment is assumed, instead the relative wage of unskilled labor in the United States falls just enough to offset the incipient reduction in demand for that type of labor. Then the United States produces (and exports) more of the good whose production is intensive in the use of skilled labor. But the theory holds that both that good and the import-competing good should now be produced with the use of relatively more of the unskilled labor than before, because its relative wage has fallen. In brief, imports of goods produced with cheaper foreign unskilled labor reduce the relative wage but increase the use of unskilled US labor.

Relaxing the constraints on full employment or allowing skill upgrading by unskilled US labor in response to the change in relative wages would reduce the force of the conclusion, but in general does not reverse it. Other models of international trade that allow for strategic business pricing and costly adjustment of capital resources yield the same forces. Similarly, some departure from the assumptions of identical tastes and technology can be absorbed without altering the fundamental forces yielding the conclusion that trade flows lead to relative price movements that are matched with relative wage changes.[3]

The theoretical trade framework shows the direction of the relationship between trade flows and relative wages, but not how strong the forces are or how large an impact they have; these measurements are the task of empirical analysis. In taking the trade models to the data, many researchers look for a link between quantity of imports and the relative wage outcome.[4] What generates the increase in imports is not defined, so these researchers often confound the role of imports of products that use unskilled labor intensively with the role of imports that are coming into the country in response to relatively more robust growth at home. On balance, this research suggests that imports have not played the principal role in changing relative wages, nor in the loss of manufacturing jobs. The modal esti-

---

3. Examples of this approach include Mann (1988) and Borjas and Ramey (1993).

4. In theory, the empirical search ought to start with a change in relative prices, since this is the engine that drives the trade flows and the subsequent change in relative wages. There are three different strands of the literature that start the process with an increase in imports. The first approach observes that imports as a share of GDP is insufficiently large to be an important determinant of the decline in relative wages. See, for example, Krugman and Lawrence (1996). For the counterproposition, namely, that wages are set on the margin, and that therefore the import share is not a valid indicator of labor-market pressures, see Leamer (1996). For the effect of import prices on wages, see Mann (1996). The second strand, often called factor-content or decomposition analysis, classifies imports by their labor content and is often used by labor economists; it is discussed later in this chapter. Examples include Borjas, Freeman, and Katz (1991), Berman, Bound, and Griliches (1994), and Wood (1995). The third strand uses cointegration regression analysis to compare the data-generating processes for the trade deficit and for the relative wage movements; see Borjas and Ramey (1994). For a fourth approach, see Cline (1997).

mates are that 10 to 20 percent of the decline in the relative wage of the unskilled worker and less than 10 percent of the decline in manufacturing jobs may be due to increased imports.

A problem with the HOS model and its empirical implementation is that, according to the model, in addition to a decline in the relative wage of the unskilled worker, there should also be a shift in demand toward unskilled labor. In reality, even though the relative wage of skilled labor has risen, the demand for and use of this type of labor also has increased (figure 4.5).

A Model of Labor Skills and Institutions, International Trade, and Wages

There are other analytical frameworks and empirical approaches to the link between trade and wages. In these models, relative wages are first and foremost a function of worker skills as proxied by experience and educational attainment and of the balance between the supply of and the demand for labor with these skills. Investigations examine whether and how much international trade shifts either the demand for or the supply of certain types of workers. They then infer the impact on relative wages of workers classified by education and/or experience.[5]

The main difficulty with this approach is that either the demand or the supply side is usually taken as given, which can generate inconsistencies and difficulties in implementation. For example, some authors say that imports shift labor demand—that is, imports reduce the demand for certain kinds of labor because consumers buy imports instead of domestically produced goods that use that kind of labor. But other researchers calculate how much labor is "embodied" in imports, and thus imports become a factor that implicitly shifts labor supply.

Research by Borjas and Ramey (1994) linking labor institutions, sectoral trade deficits, and relative wages offers the foundation for a possible relationship between the widening trade deficit and the falling household savings rate. Further research is necessary to test this relationship, but it could work as follows. Borjas and Ramey show that the bulk of the widening of the trade deficit from 1963 to 1988 was in highly concentrated industries in the manufacturing sector. Workers in these sectors often earn wages well above those commensurate with their level of skill or education, in part because the highly concentrated industries redistribute some of their economic profits back to workers (in some cases, to avoid strikes).

---

5. Examples of this work include Bound and Johnson (1992), Berman, Bound, and Griliches (1994), Murphy and Welch (1991, 1992), Feenstra and Hanson (1995), and Brauer and Hickok (1995).

Figure 4.5 Relative wages and relative employment of skilled and unskilled workers

A. Change in average wage premium to skilled worker

percentage

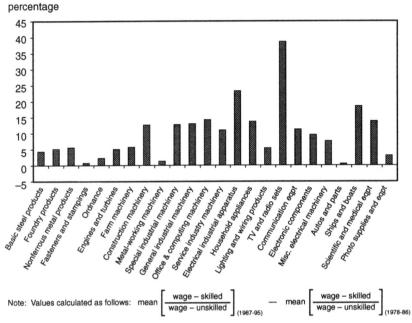

Note: Values calculated as follows: $\text{mean}\left[\dfrac{\text{wage} - \text{skilled}}{\text{wage} - \text{unskilled}}\right]_{(1987\text{-}95)} - \text{mean}\left[\dfrac{\text{wage} - \text{skilled}}{\text{wage} - \text{unskilled}}\right]_{(1978\text{-}86)}$

B. Change in average relative employment of skilled worker

percentage

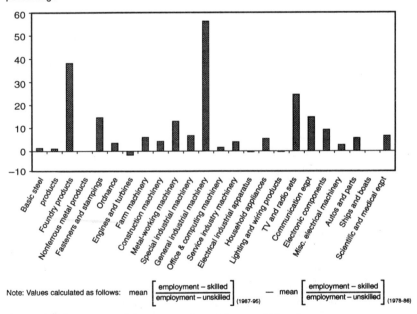

Note: Values calculated as follows: $\text{mean}\left[\dfrac{\text{employment} - \text{skilled}}{\text{employment} - \text{unskilled}}\right]_{(1987\text{-}95)} - \text{mean}\left[\dfrac{\text{employment} - \text{skilled}}{\text{employment} - \text{unskilled}}\right]_{(1978\text{-}86)}$

Source: US Department of Commerce, Annual Survey of Manufactures.

As jobs were lost in these sectors, workers moved into other sectors where wages more closely matched skills, and their path of lifetime income fell.[6]

Because consumption paths change relatively slowly, if permanent income falls, the household savings rate would also tend to fall. If a sufficiently large group of workers were displaced from jobs where they earned a sufficient wage to be both spenders and moderate savers and went into jobs at lower wages where they were zero savers, it could help explain the relationship between the widening trade deficit and the falling household savings rate. Since we know that there are many more jobs being created in the US economy that are at the high-skill, high-wage end of the spectrum, the challenge is to figure out how to move displaced workers into these job opportunities. Skill upgrading could have the triple benefit of narrowing the trade gap, raising worker incomes, and increasing the household savings rate.

Trade and Technology Go Hand in Hand

Most of the empirical studies on the determination of relative wages explain only about half or less of the change in relative wages. Many researchers call the unexplained factor "technological change" or "productivity growth." They then opine that technology must have a more important effect on relative wages than trade has.

Going back to the theory offers few insights on what additional variables or data might improve the empirical analysis, either to reduce the unexplained residual or explicitly to model technology (see Collins 1985, Leamer 1994, and Richardson 1995). By itself, technical change that economizes on the use of labor releases proportionately more unskilled labor than skilled labor, yielding the decline in the relative wage of unskilled labor necessary to employ fully both types of labor.[7] Hence in theoretical models, trade and technology have the same effect.

More recent empirical work recognizes that technology both drives and is driven by international trade. Hence empirical analysis that includes only trade data but not technology data will yield biased estimates of the role of trade for relative wage movements. Moreover, this new work also recognizes that exports, not just imports, might affect relative wages; indeed, much of the earlier empirical work on trade and relative wages actually only examines imports.

This new analysis suggests complex relationships between trade, productivity growth, and relative wages. International discipline can affect

---

6. For more discussion of the consequences of job displacement and the relationship between trade and job displacement, see Kletzer (1998a, 1998b).

7. The only key assumption for this result is that the production function for the low-skill good is relatively more intensive in the use of unskilled labor.

Table 4.2 Impact of trade exposure on relative wages
(regression coefficients, sample of 21 industries)

Technology factor	0.7	(not significant)
Initial exposure[a]		
Exports	0.6	
Imports	-0.2	(not significant)
Changes in exposure[b]		
Exports	1.6	
Imports	-0.6	(not significant)

Note: Vector of change in mean relative wage defined as in figure 4.5.
a. Share of exports in production and imports in domestic consumption at beginning of sample period (1978).
b. Change in average exposure between first and second half of sample period ([1995-87] − [1978-86]).

Source: Mann (1997).

firms and their workers in two ways: initial exposure and change in exposure to global trade. On the import side, an increase in imports can show firms what new varieties of products are available, and reverse engineering can communicate new technologies. However, rising imports may not pressure firms into changing the way they do business if at the same time the domestic market also is expanding. Firms may not even recognize that they are in competition until they start losing market share to imports. Similarly, on the export side, simply committing to try to export can encourage technological uptake and best practice. Firms do not have to have a larger share of exports in the production run to benefit from export competition.

When researchers take these hypotheses about trade competition to the data and control for the trade-productivity relationship, they find that it is *export* competition for *foreign* markets that has the more powerful effect on relative wages, not *import* competition in the *domestic* market (table 4.2) (Mann 1997, 1998). That is, when interactions between trade and productivity growth are controlled for, the exposure of industry to exports emerges as the more important force driving the increased wage premium to skilled workers. This suggests that, in contrast to common belief and to most previous research, it is not so much that import competition is bidding down the wages of the unskilled worker, but that demand for skilled labor is bidding up the wages of skilled workers. It is the commitment to export and, in particular, an increased share of exports in production that are associated with strong relative-wage effects. Import exposure is not a significant determinant of the change in the skilled-unskilled wage premium over the 1980s and 1990s.[8]

---

8. The results are consistent with the conclusions on wage premia from Katz and Summers (1995) and Richardson and Rindal (1996), and match quite well with the results of Bernard and Jensen (1997).

In addition to helping to explain the behavior of relative wages, the complex relationship between trade and productivity growth has important implications for the long-term sustainable rate of growth of the US economy, a topic to which we turn in the next chapter. From the standpoint of policy initiatives, it seems clear that skill and flexibility training will allow workers to take advantage of job opportunities in the expanding sectors.

Yet, despite the expanding corpus of research showing that technology-driven demand for skilled workers raises the skill premium, the political sensitivity to import competition remains, as reflected in legislation to assist workers in transition and to protect some industries. There is thus a potential conflict between the demand for less—or at least less rapid—integration with global markets because of the perceived consequences for some workers, and the benefits that such integration confers on the economy as a whole. Managing this conflict has important implications for the sustainability of the external deficit, not because of simple economics but because of the much more complex relationships between social well-being and politics.

Conclusion

Summary

■ Political rhetoric often emphasizes the relationship between the globalization of the US economy and the dynamics of the US labor market. The relationship actually has two facets, one associated with changes in the *trade balance* and the other with changes in *export and import flows,* the components of the trade balance.

■ From the perspective of the overall economy and the overall labor market, it is clear that a trade deficit is driven by expenditure greater than production at home and by faster growth at home than abroad. A trade deficit widens when US growth is good and job opportunities abound, and it shrinks when a recession occurs and unemployment rises.

■ Several theoretical models of the relationship between trade flows and relative wages suggest that increased trade with low-skill and low-wage countries will have a negative effect on the wages of low-skilled American workers. However, these models yield the same conclusions when technological change is substituted for trade.

■ In empirical analysis, when trade flows, productivity growth, and relative wages are all considered together, a complex relationship emerges among them. It is increasingly apparent that trade and productivity growth work hand in hand to raise the relative wages of skilled workers by increasing the demand for such workers.

Policy Discussion

■ The policy focus that emerges from the research places emphasis squarely on education and on skill and flexibility training of workers so that they can take advantage of job opportunities in the expanding sectors, whether these be at import-competing firms with enhanced technology or exporting firms serving the international marketplace.

■ Trade policies that limit flows of imports of a certain set of industries would do little to reduce wage dispersion, but could reduce productivity growth and thus undermine the long-term potential of the US economy, to the detriment of all workers.

■ A final reason to focus on policies that will improve the distribution of wages is somewhat speculative: The increase in wage dispersion correlates to some degree with the downward trend in household savings and the downward trend in the trade balance. If a policy plan could improve the economic fortunes of less skilled workers, it might have the additional beneficial effect of improving the rate of household savings, and closing the current account gap.

5

What Role for Trade in the "New Paradigm" of Sustainable Long-Run Growth?

Productivity growth is the key variable . . . in the economy's long-run growth performance. . . . [T]echnology, globalization, a balanced budget, and enhanced educational attainment may increase productivity growth . . . in the years to come . . . and nurture smoother growth over time.

—Laura D'Andrea Tyson, "Just How New Is the 'New Economy'?"
Business Week (1 June 1998)

The dollar's strength . . . has helped to hold down inflation and has lent support to the theory that America was undergoing an economic miracle . . . [but] virtuous circles can easily turn vicious.

—*Economist* (19 January 1999)

As the economy expanded in the late 1990s, US economic performance outstripped expectations year after year with lower unemployment, faster growth in output, lower price inflation, growing incomes, and soaring wealth. Most observers of the macroeconomy did not believe that this combination could continue for so long. Inevitably, they said, robust growth would lead to higher inflation, as it had in virtually every other economic cycle observed since World War II (figure 5.1). Higher inflation generally precipitates a tightening of the money supply by the Federal Reserve, which slows growth. But with price inflation quiescent, the

Figure 5.1 Growth, inflation, and recessions, 1960-98

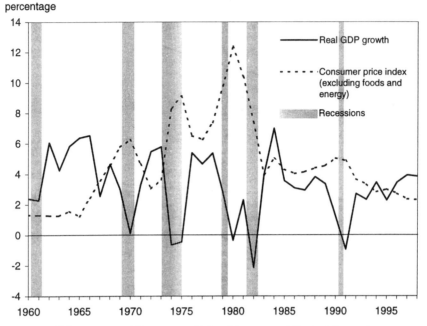

percentage

Federal Reserve has not tightened monetary policy since mid-1994—and indeed, it loosened monetary policy in 1998 in reaction to the global financial turmoil and its potential impact on the US economy. Is there a "new paradigm" of macroeconomic activity in which the relationship between too-rapid growth and inflation no longer applies—or has this trade-off been masked by a fortuitous combination of factors? What role does globalization play in either altering the parameters of the old relationship or creating the new paradigm?

The Trade-Off between Inflation and Unemployment

The notion that there is a trade-off between price inflation and the rate of growth of output comes from a 1958 article by the British economist A. W. Phillips, who observed that there was a negative relationship between wage inflation and the unemployment rate in UK data from 1861 to 1957; that is, as unemployment fell, the wage inflation rate tended to rise. Since then a number of new ideas have modified the simple relationship that

Phillips first presented.[1] The more recent theories focus on the supply side of the economy. Events such as the oil price shocks of the 1970s are integrated into the analysis; the impact of labor-market policies such as welfare and unemployment compensation are considered; and understanding of the psychology of wage and price formation and of the role of expectations has been deepened.

In fact, there are two distinct relationships between inflation and resource utilization that need to be analyzed—one within the labor market, such as that observed by Phillips, and the other in the general economy between a broad measure of price inflation (such as the consumer price index [CPI] or GDP deflator) and the rate of growth of GDP. Some analysts argue that this distinction is unnecessary—that whenever labor costs rise, prices cannot be far behind. These analysts suggest that a single parameter of labor-market tightness, such as the unemployment rate, is sufficient to pin down the relationship between price inflation and output growth. This parameter is often called the "nonaccelerating inflation rate of unemployment" (NAIRU) or sometimes the "natural rate of unemployment." Below this rate of unemployment wage costs tend to rise, which often causes price inflation to accelerate.

The rationale for the trade-off between wage increases and the unemployment rate comes from simple supply-and-demand analysis. If more labor is demanded by firms, then its "price"—that is, wages—will rise. The concept of the NAIRU, however, suggests that this relationship is not linear: As unemployment falls further and further, firms find it increasingly difficult to find labor to meet their needs, and hence the compensation they are willing to pay rises at an accelerating rate. That said, the NAIRU is not a fixed and unchanging unemployment rate. Labor-market policies, such as the generosity of unemployment compensation, clearly affect the NAIRU, as does the match between the skills workers have and the skills firms need.[2] Nevertheless, if the NAIRU changes only slowly over time, and if there is a tight relationship between wage inflation and price inflation, then the NAIRU can help in predicting price inflation in the future.

The 1990s data contain several interrelated puzzles, however, that call into question the assumption that there always is a tight relationship between wage inflation and price inflation. On the one hand, as illustrated in figure 5.2a, the negative relationship between the change in average hourly earnings (wages) and the unemployment rate is still in evidence.

---

1. For a general discussion of the Phillips curve and new theories of aggregate supply, see any modern macroeconomics textbook (e.g., Mankiw 1997, 346ff.).

2. See chapter 4 for a discussion of how trade may affect the relative wages of workers with different kinds of skills. See OECD (1996) for more discussion of social policy and the NAIRU.

Figure 5.2 Puzzles in 1990s inflation-output relationship

A. Unemployment rate and average hourly earnings

average hourly earnings
(year-over-year, 1990-98, monthly data, percentage)

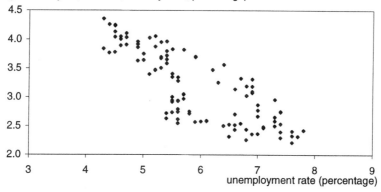

B. Real GDP growth and inflation

core CPI (year-over-year, 1990-98, quarterly data, percentages)

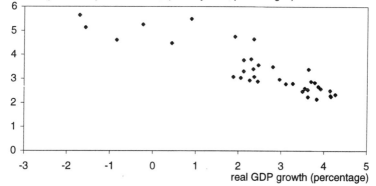

C. Inflation and GDP growth

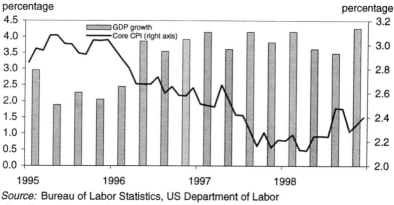

Source: Bureau of Labor Statistics, US Department of Labor
<http://stats.bls.gov:80/datahome.htm>.

But the rise in labor costs in the past several years has not been passed through to increase price inflation. Hence when the Phillips curve is respecified to the more general relationship between the price inflation rate and the rate of growth of output, as shown in figure 5.2b, the negative relationship is not so clearly and cleanly observed. Indeed, as figure 5.2c illustrates, price inflation has generally fallen even as GDP growth has remained strong (and unemployment low) over the past several years.

What factors, then, might be loosening the link between wages and prices, and between prices and output growth? Are those factors temporary or permanent? What role do international factors in particular play?

New Investment and the Inflation-Output Trade-Off

Just as strong employment growth tends to push up wage inflation, high rates of utilization of industrial capacity tend to push up price inflation. However, investment in the United States has been particularly robust during this expansion. While the narrowing of the federal budget deficit has been important in releasing funds for productive investment, so too has the additional finance provided by foreign savings (see chapter 2, especially figure 2.5).

The additional physical capital provided by investment has meant that the additional labor employed in recent years has had sufficient plant and equipment to produce effectively. Without the additional capital, capacity utilization might have risen into an inflationary zone. In fact, new research (Corrado and Mattey 1997) suggests that the nonaccelerating inflation rate of capacity utilization (NAIRCU) is just as important a concept for understanding the dynamics of the relationship between price inflation and output growth as the NAIRU concept is for labor, the other major input to the production process.[3]

Moreover, a key component of the investment surge in the last half of the 1990s has been in computers and other information technology equipment (Sichel 1999). Real net investment in computers and peripheral equipment rose more than 40 percent per year between 1996 and 1998, and the real net capital stock rose 37 percent. As of 1998, computers accounted for more than 40 percent of the total nominal nonresidential stock of investment. Such remarkable growth was powered by prices calculated to be falling at an average rate of nearly 30 percent per year. As discussed

3. Some analysts have held in recent years that too much investment in plant and equipment has been undertaken around the world. To be sure, when economies in much of the world are growing at rates well below what they are capable of, it will appear that there is too much capacity. Paul Krugman (1997) effectively points out the mistaken thinking underlying the "global glut."

in chapter 3, one reason that prices have been falling so fast is the globalization of production of computers and related equipment.

International Forces and the Inflation-Output Trade-Off

Other international factors have contributed to falling inflation rates in recent years. The dollar has appreciated, contributing to downward pressures on input costs as well as on final goods prices. Commodity prices have weakened, in particular on account of the slow growth in other parts of the world. Finally, the growing market clout of imports has increased competition in the domestic marketplace, further keeping prices in check. And the drive to expand into markets abroad has made exporters acutely conscious of pricing. Some of these international forces should be temporary, and others may be more lasting.

First, the trade-weighted exchange value of the dollar appreciated some 25 percent from mid-1995 through mid-1999. To varying extents and with varying delays, firms pass exchange rate changes through to their prices,[4] and thus the appreciation of the dollar tended to reduce import prices (figure 5.3).

In addition, commodity prices have been falling, particularly as growth has slowed abroad but also because technological change has increased the efficiency of, and lowered the cost of, extraction and production (World Bank 1999). On the export side, sales abroad have had to contend not only with an appreciating dollar but also with sluggish activity in other economies. Export prices declined particularly sharply in 1997 and 1998 until the dollar began to depreciate late in the year.

The falling import prices and falling commodity prices have slowed the rate of price inflation. Different measures of price inflation have slowed to differing degrees with the different behavior directly related to international trade exposure and competition. Inflation has come down the most in those sectors with the greatest exposure to international competition. For example, producers of manufactured goods face competition from imports that account for about 30 percent of their domestic market, and 25 percent of their sales are destined for foreign markets. With such fierce competition at home and for markets abroad, it is not surprising that producer prices rose only very slowly over the past few years. (The depreciation of the dollar in the second half of 1998 lessened some of the compet-

---

4. For an example and further discussion of the relationship between the exchange value of the dollar and the competitiveness of US products, see chapter 7 (esp. table 7.1). On average, about 60 percent of an exchange rate change is passed through to a change in import prices; about one-half of the total amount occurs in the contemporaneous quarter and the rest over the subsequent three quarters.

Figure 5.3 International influences and price inflation

A. Dollar exchange rate, import and export prices

percentage change from previous year

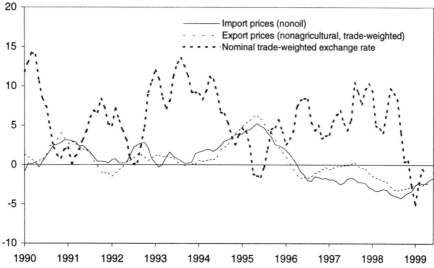

Sources: Bureau of Labor Statistics, *Export and Import Prices;* IMF, *International Financial Statistics.*

B. Inflation rates

percentage change from previous year

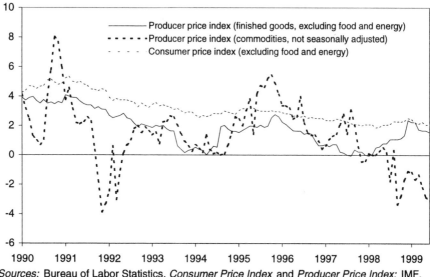

Sources: Bureau of Labor Statistics, *Consumer Price Index* and *Producer Price Index;* IMF, *International Financial Statistics.*

itive pressure, and the PPI for finished goods, excluding food and energy, tipped back up in late 1998—see figure 5.3.)

For consumers as well, international competition has been a key force dampening price inflation. About 50 percent of consumer goods (excluding automobiles) are imported, so this component of consumer price inflation has been trending downward. In addition, the dampening force of international prices and competition matter even for the broadest measure of consumer price inflation, in which domestic services account for 60 percent. Wages, which are particularly important in the labor-intensive service-sector industries, are rising less quickly than they otherwise would because of the slowed rate of consumer price inflation. Thus international factors are integral to the "virtuous" circle of lower inflation (Mann 1996).

All told, the declines in import prices might have cut about 1.8 percentage points off CPI inflation since 1996, more than accounting for the decline in inflation. At some point the rest of the world will return to a more normal growth path, releasing some of the downward pressure on import prices and offering some upward price flexibility both to producers of domestic-competing goods and to exporters. In addition, pressure on the dollar to depreciate will likely intensify (see chapter 10). From the point of view of the long-term trade-off between inflation and output, how much of the benefits of international competition is likely to remain, and how much is fleeting and dependent on changes in exchange rates and business cycles here and abroad?

Globalization and Trend Productivity Growth

There are two ways an economy can increase output. One of these is to use more resources, such as labor and capital. Once these resources are fully employed, however, further noninflationary increases in output must come from improvements in the utilization of resources. Such improvements often are measured as increases in *trend* productivity growth. A higher rate of productivity growth should increase the maximum growth rate that an economy can achieve without accelerating the rate of inflation. In addition, higher productivity growth implies that firms can afford to raise wages, maintain prices, and yet avoid too hard a hit on their profit rate. Thus an increase in the trend rate of productivity growth would help resolve the constellation of puzzling data observed in the late 1990s.

But has trend productivity growth increased? It is difficult to measure productivity growth, and even more difficult to determine whether *trend* productivity growth has changed. It is well known that productivity varies over the business cycle. For example, as demand for their goods rises, firms initially work their existing resources harder (e.g., with overtime or speeded-up production runs) to produce more output. Productivity (output divided by inputs) increases, but firms cannot forever work their employees and machines harder to generate more output; they must ultimately work them more efficiently and effectively. It is this second type of productivity gain, measured by changes in *trend* productivity growth, that generates increased sustainable growth in GDP.

Whether trend productivity growth over the 1990s has increased remains controversial. However, there is no question that productivity growth has been more rapid for the manufacturing sector of the economy (figure 5.4). For the broader aggregate, the nonfarm business sector, a higher average productivity growth apparently has been maintained for the latter half of the 1990s; this may be due only to the manufacturing component or it may suggest a new, higher trend for the whole economy.[5]

In any case, the manufacturing sector is more exposed than the service sector to international competition; this suggests a key relationship between international competition and faster productivity growth. Within the manufacturing sector, there is substantial variation in both productivity growth and exposure to international trade and competition. This variation in productivity growth across industries can be used as a laboratory of sorts for investigating whether international forces may be an important ingredient in raising productivity growth.

There are two channels through which trade can affect trend productivity growth: changes in volume of output and changes in competition. The first is quite familiar from the work of many macroeconomists on aggregate productivity data. Productivity tends to be "procyclical," rising and falling as demand and output rise and fall. In the global environment, increased demand for exports should raise overall output and increase productivity. On the other hand, unless domestic demand stays strong, an increase in imports would tend to reduce productivity growth as imports substitute for domestic consumption and reduce domestic output.

The second channel, competition, has to do with the relative share of imports in domestic consumption and of exports in production. Research shows that information conveyed to firms from trade competition is different from that conveyed through competition with other domestic firms and can stimulate a change in trend productivity growth. For example, imported goods can be reverse engineered, during which firms learn about new production techniques. In addition, if among import-competing firms some are more efficient and cost-effective producers, these firms will survive import competition longer than other firms. Thus the least productive firms exit, leaving the more productive firms to raise the overall average. On the export side, firms that export a higher fraction of their product could have a more flexible and efficient production technology, which increases their ability to meet foreign designs and demand; reverse engi-

---

5. Corrado and Slifman (1996) examine productivity and output data for a broad set of manufacturing and service-sector data and also discuss issues of measurement. See also Gordon (1999) for another view of productivity growth and the "new paradigm."

Figure 5.4 Labor productivity growth and trends

A. Labor productivity, 1960-98

1960 = 100

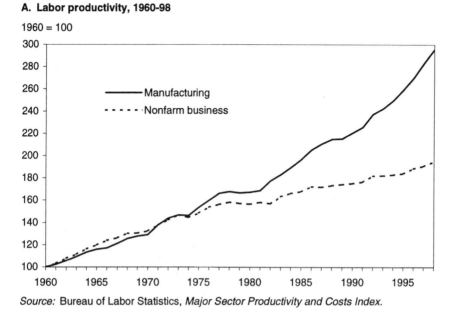

Source: Bureau of Labor Statistics, *Major Sector Productivity and Costs Index.*

B. Nonfarm business productivity growth trend, 1947-98

1960 = 100

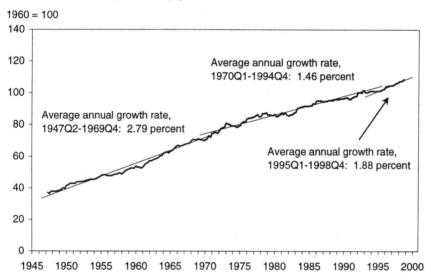

Table 5.1 Trade and productivity growth (regression coefficients, sample of 21 industries)

Effect on trend productivity growth[a]	
Volume effect[b]	
Domestic shipments	0.55
Imports	-0.13
Exports	0.34
Competition effect[b]	
Imports	0.6
Exports	-0.55 (not significant)

a. Vector of change in trend productivity growth is measured as mean[total factor productivity]$_{1995-87}$ – mean[total factor productivity]$_{1978-86}$.
b. Change in average of sample variable between first and second half of sample period: (1995-87) – (1978-86).

Source: Mann (1998).

neering is important for exporters as well. Moreover, much evidence suggests that firms that export are more productive than firms that do not (Richardson and Rindal 1995, 1996).

Systematic analysis of a cross-section of manufacturing industries reveals that importing and exporting raise trend productivity growth but with different weights on the two channels (table 5.1). Before considering the effect of international factors, however, it is clear that the domestic market remains very important for manufacturers' productivity growth. The volume effect on productivity growth coming from changes in domestic shipments to domestic customers is greater than the volume effect coming from increased imports or increased exports. This is not surprising since on balance US manufacturers still have very large domestic markets.

Consider now the volume and competition effects of international trade. On the import side, the volume effect has the expected relationship: rising volume of imports apparently reduces the domestic volume produced, with negative consequences for productivity growth. But this volume effect is countered by a much stronger positive effect on trend productivity growth coming from the competition effect. When imports begin to take over the domestic market, and when domestic firms must fight for market share, trend productivity growth increases. On the other hand, on the export side, expanding sales abroad (the volume effect) appear to have the more important role in affecting productivity. Simply raising the share of exports in the production run (the competition effect) does not appear to raise productivity further (Mann 1998).

Globalization also may affect productivity growth through its synergy with spending on research and development (Baygan and Mann 1999).

R&D and trade can work together to raise productivity growth in two ways. First, R&D innovations in one country can "spill over" into another via trade flows, as in the case of reverse engineering. The firms in the recipient country adopt innovations and learn best practice, which increases productivity growth. In another model of the R&D and trade relationship, the forces of international competition encourage firms within a country to undertake R&D spending so as to improve the efficiency of resource usage within that country. Research that aggregates industries into different groups on the basis of the degree of technological sophistication suggests that R&D spending does raise productivity growth, but only when trade encourages and diffuses the fullest uptake of globally available technological innovations by all firms within an industry.

In sum, research indicates that globalization changes the way in which resources are used in the US economy. Moreover, the globalization of computer production contributes to a greater integration of computers and information technology into the capital stock that is available to the economy at large, not just to that portion of the economy exposed to international forces. Consequently, productivity gains occur not only because of the direct forces of the international marketplace through competition and demand but also because of the indirect benefits that accrue to purely domestic producers in their use of products that are made cheaper and better by globalization. These forces of international trade appear to have produced permanent changes in the way the US economy works, allowing GDP growth to remain above 3.5 percent with inflation below 2 percent for more than three years.

Conclusion

Summary

■ Over the last half of the 1990s, US growth has been particularly robust while inflation has fallen. During every other postwar expansion there has been a positive relationship between output growth and inflation—robust growth has generally led to increased price inflation. While the positive relationship has not been eliminated, it has been both masked and fundamentally changed by globalization.

■ International forces, some temporary and others more enduring, have helped to alter the relationship. First, the appreciation of the dollar has kept down import prices. In addition, slow global growth has kept commodity prices low. Finally, slack demand in overseas markets has put downward pressure on export prices. At some point, these temporary factors will reverse. The dollar will depreciate, import prices will no longer dampen domestic inflation, and export prices could rise.

Global growth will resume, boosting commodity prices, foreign costs and prices, and domestic prices.

■ However, stiffer international competition, both on the import and on the export side, have made producers acutely aware of pricing, have enhanced productivity growth, and may have made R&D spending even more beneficial. Moreover, foreign savings have helped to finance new investment in plant and equipment in the United States, which allows US firms to hire more labor without running into capacity constraints. And, finally, the benefits of globalized production of computers are filtering through to enhance resource utilization in all industries and services. Even when the temporary factors recede, these permanent benefits of globalization for long-term sustainable growth will remain.

Policy Discussion

■ From the standpoint of economic analysis, the policy implications are becoming familiar. International forces are allowing the current robust expansion to continue and are enhancing the long-term ability of the United States to grow without generating inflation. Restricting trade would have a negative effect on both the short-run and the long-run performance of the economy.

■ Moreover, there are important synergies between open trade, global investment, and the effectiveness of R&D spending. The ability of firms to decompose the production and service processes and to invest and trade worldwide is key to generating productivity gains and lower inflation. Efforts to keep R&D at home or to prevent industry from investing abroad will obviate the very benefits such policies were thought to confer on selected industries or groups of workers.

■ These insights have not been wholly understood by the population at large or embraced by many of their elected representatives. As noted in the previous chapter, adjustment by firms and workers to economic dynamics is not without cost. In addition to creating policies that facilitate adjustment, it is important that we describe and quantify the benefits of globalization. Lower inflation rates benefit all people, especially those who consume a large fraction of their income. Faster productivity growth is the foundation for higher wages and allows monetary policy makers to keep interest rates low for longer periods without being concerned about inflation. Increasing the size of the economic pie through productivity growth offers higher levels of economic well-being to everyone; policies of education, training, and flexibility ensure that everyone can take advantage of those opportunities.

III

How Do Competitiveness and Trade Policy Affect Sustainability?

6

Is the External Deficit Caused by Unfair Trade Practices?

The US trade deficit is at an all-time high because of our government's irresponsible trade policy. . . . [O]ur inability to insist on fair trade, especially with China, is forcing us down the wrong path.

—US Representative Sherrod Brown (D-OH), press release (17 July 1998)

But use of the trade balance as a measure of the success of market-opening endeavors is problematic. Changes in the trade balance are seldom related to specific market-opening efforts; indeed, the trade balance is generally determined by macroeconomic factors, not microeconomic barriers to trade.

—Council of Economic Advisers, *Economic Report of the President* (1998)

Most people agree that the US market is the most open in the world. It is equally clear that US exports face trade barriers in some foreign markets. If US exports face particularly high barriers in a certain country, it seems reasonable to think that the United States could have a bilateral trade deficit with that country, particularly if US consumers bought a lot of imports from the country. If such a bilateral deficit is quite large, it seems reasonable to think that reducing specific barriers facing US exports in that market would not only reduce that bilateral deficit but also would reduce the US overall trade deficit and contribute to the sustainability of the current account.

There are several fallacies in this reasoning. First, trade relationships between countries depend foremost on resource endowments and tastes, on relative costs of production, and on technological choices, not on trade barriers (see chapter 3). Countries produce and demand different "baskets of goods" from each other; why should these baskets of goods and services be of equal value between all country pairs? Second, countries are not of the same economic size. Small countries might export a lot of a particular commodity to a large country like the United States, but buy only a small amount of a specialized service in return. The small country likely trades with several countries, not just the United States, to obtain the full range of products that it needs. Third, countries are at different stages of economic development, and hence demand different sets of products than any single country, such as the United States, has to offer. Finally, at any point in time, some countries could be in recession and therefore will import less. Given this range of variability, bilateral imbalances are almost an inevitable outcome of different resource endowments, tastes, levels of development, and cycles of economic activity; a zero bilateral trade account is rare indeed.

That said, *persistent* and large or increasing bilateral deficits that are not related to unique endowments may indicate barriers to US exports, particularly if a country is persistently in surplus with all of its trading partners and if the domestic prices of the products in question are far above the world price.[1] In any case, the magnitude of bilateral deficits, particularly when concentrated in certain industries, generates both politically heated debate and calls for protection or retaliation from the affected industries in the United States.

Reducing the barriers facing particular US exports in overseas markets certainly increases trade flows and helps the affected industries. But the key question in this chapter is whether such a change in specific barriers abroad and even specific bilateral trade imbalances would change the *overall* external imbalance. Chapter 2 showed that the US external imbalance comes from the difference between savings and investment in the United States. In order for bilateral trade negotiations with an individual trading partner to have an impact on the overall external balance, it must work through either the savings or the investment channel.

Sources of Bilateral Deficits

Trade Theory

Trade theory provides the underpinnings of how much and what kinds of products countries will trade with each other when all of a country's resources are fully and efficiently employed. The basic principle, as noted in

---

1. If the domestic price of a product is well above the world price for the product, it suggests that trade is being restricted. Free trade would add supply, and the domestic price would tend to fall.

Figure 6.1 Trade patterns and bilateral balances

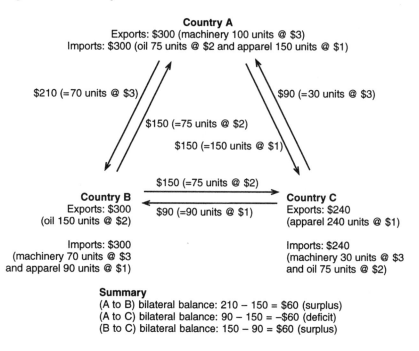

Country A
Exports: $300 (machinery 100 units @ $3)
Imports: $300 (oil 75 units @ $2 and apparel 150 units @ $1)

$210 (=70 units @ $3)

$90 (=30 units @ $3)

$150 (=75 units @ $2)

$150 (=150 units @ $1)

$150 (=75 units @ $2)

Country B
Exports: $300
(oil 150 units @ $2)

$90 (=90 units @ $1)

Country C
Exports: $240
(apparel 240 units @ $1)

Imports: $300
(machinery 70 units @ $3
and apparel 90 units @ $1)

Imports: $240
(machinery 30 units @ $3
and oil 75 units @ $2)

Summary
(A to B) bilateral balance: 210 − 150 = $60 (surplus)
(A to C) bilateral balance: 90 − 150 = −$60 (deficit)
(B to C) bilateral balance: 150 − 90 = $60 (surplus)

chapter 3, is that a country exports those products for which it is a particularly well-suited producer—that is, for which it has comparative advantage. Can differences in comparative advantage lead to bilateral imbalances?

Figure 6.1 illustrates a simple example. Suppose there are three countries—A, B, and C—and three goods—machinery, oil, and apparel. Firms specialize in production of the good in which the country has the comparative advantage and export some of it. Country A has the comparative advantage in machinery and exports 100 units at $3 each. Country B has the comparative advantage in oil and exports 150 units at $2 each. Country C has the comparative advantage in apparel and exports 240 units at $1 each. Households in each country want to consume some of each good. Suppose each country's *overall* trade balance is zero, so the value of exports equals the value of imports. Country A imports 75 units of oil and 150 units of apparel. Country B imports 70 units of machinery and 90 units of apparel. Country C imports 30 units of machinery and 75 units of oil.

Although each country's *overall* trade account is balanced, none of the *bilateral* trade accounts are in balance. Country A (the United States?) has a bilateral surplus with country B (Venezuela?) and a bilateral deficit with country C (China?). Similar bilateral imbalances characterize the flows between the other two countries. The bilateral imbalances arise in this simple example because we have assumed differences in comparative advantage but similarities in tastes.

Macroeconomic Factors

Countries' trade flows and balances also are affected by the level of macroeconomic activity and relative prices.[2] Suppose one country is growing quickly and consuming a lot of imports while its trading partners languish in the doldrums of their business cycles and import only a little. The bilateral trade flows will be unbalanced so long as the two countries are at different points in their business cycles. Even when countries operate at full employment and full capacity utilization (referred to as "potential output"), bilateral imbalances could remain, for the reasons discussed above.

Another macroeconomic factor that will affect a country's overall and bilateral trade flows and balances is a change in the relative price between two countries' products (export price relative to price of competing goods abroad and import price relative to competing goods at home).[3] Suppose that the home currency depreciates against the currency of a trading partner. All else unchanged, this depreciation would tend to make exports more price competitive in the destination market of the trading partner, and import-competing goods more price competitive against the products purchased from the trading partner. Exports to that partner would tend to rise, imports from that partner would tend to fall, and the bilateral balance would tend toward a surplus. However, only if the home currency depreciation were against the currencies of all the trading partners would the overall trade account tend toward surplus.

A third macroeconomic explanation depends on demographics. Over an individual's stylized life cycle, there is first birth; second, a period of earning, saving, and buildup of wealth; and finally, a period of retirement during which consumption draws on the portfolio of wealth. A similar theory based on demographics has been constructed for countries, one version of which is called the "intertemporal balance of payments" theory. A country with a working but aging population and a low birthrate and low immigration rate (Japan, for example) might reasonably be expected to have a high savings rate that yields a buildup of domestic and international assets that provides consumption to the population after the bulk of it retires. By this reasoning, a persistent trade surplus for an aging country could make sense.[4]

2. Chapter 8 provides a full discussion of this model and how it pertains to the US external imbalance.

3. For a more detailed look at how exchange rate changes pass through to change relative prices, see figure 7.1.

4. See Mankiw (1997, 420-25) for a presentation of the life-cycle model, and Obstfeld and Rogoff (1995) for a more specific presentation of the intertemporal theory of the balance of payments.

However, fallacies of the life-cycle model for the individual are compounded when the model is adapted to the country: How likely is it that a country will have no more-efficient workers (which is like having new workers)? And how likely is it that the population will all retire simultaneously? Hence, while these theories may help to explain a persistent global trade imbalance, they are not a reasonable first step for understanding bilateral imbalances.

These examples of comparative advantage and macroeconomic determinants suggest that there are many forces underlying both bilateral and overall trade patterns and balances. Separating out the particular effect of unfair trade policies would be quite difficult.

Characteristics of US Bilateral Deficits

An examination of several bilateral deficits of the United States shows that some are related exclusively to endowments and tastes, some to levels of development, some to cycles of economic activity—and some are hard to explain using these models. The US bilateral balances with most industrial-country trading partners mimic the behavior of the overall trade balance, suggesting that relative growth rates and relative prices have the key roles in driving these bilateral trade balances. In the US bilateral balances with major developing-country trading partners, in contrast, differences in comparative advantage based on stage of development as well as structural or policy factors such as trade barriers and exchange-rate management may be more important.

Canada and the European Union (EU) are broadly similar to the United States in terms of level of industrialization, resources, and, to some extent, tastes. The US bilateral balances for goods and services with Canada and the EU behave similarly to the overall US trade deficit (figure 6.2a). These bilateral balances widen when US growth is relatively stronger than growth in these trading partners. Exchange rate fluctuations also have an important effect on the US balance with the EU.

On the other hand, China as well as the Philippines, Thailand, Malaysia, and Indonesia (which, with others, collectively comprise the "Other Asia" category in figure 6.2b) are dissimilar from the United States in level of development and in tastes as well as in the types of products that can be profitably produced there. Following the simple three-country example above, we should expect US bilateral trade with these countries and regions to be unbalanced, with US imports from the region exceeding exports by a persistent amount. Indeed, we observe this in the data.

However, a notable feature of the data on the US trade balance with the Asian newly industrialized economies (NIEs)—Hong Kong, Singapore, South Korea, and Taiwan—is that the pattern is similar not to that of the

Figure 6.2 US bilateral balances, 1980-98

A. US bilateral balance on goods and services

billions of US dollars

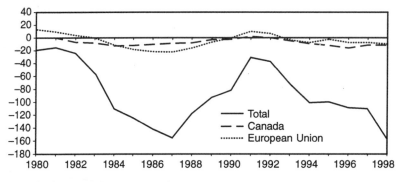

B. US bilateral balance on goods

billions of US dollars

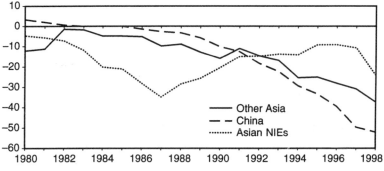

C. US bilateral balance with Japan and Mexico

billions of US dollars

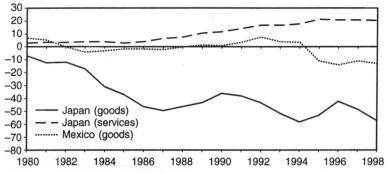

NIEs = newly industrialized economies

Note: The "European Union" category includes Austria, Belgium, Denmark, Finland, France, Germany, Greece, Ireland, Italy, Luxembourg, Netherlands, Portugal, Spain, Sweden, and United Kingdom. The "Other Asia" category covers Asia excluding Japan, China, and the Asian NIEs.

The trade balances for services for China, the NIEs, the "Other Asia" category, and Mexico are not available.

Source: US Department of Commerce, *International Transactions Tables.*

United States with China and the "Other Asia" countries but to that of the United States with Canada and the EU.

In 1980 the Asian NIEs were classified as developing economies by most measures. Now, on the basis of per capita income, all four are comfortably within the OECD range, and two rank well above the OECD average. These countries exemplify the argument that a movement along the path of economic development erodes the persistent trade imbalances with the United States. As the Asian NIEs developed, their comparative advantage changed (with much production moving to China) and their consumers' demand for the sophisticated products and services of the United States increased. For both reasons, their trade deficits with the United States narrowed (and the US deficit with China increased). The speed with which this transition has taken place in these Asian economies is remarkable. While the financial turmoil and exchange rate changes of 1997 and 1998 affected US trade with the region and the purchasing power of Asian incomes, this development path (and pattern of trade) is assured and will be resumed.

In addition to the bilateral imbalance with China, two other bilateral US imbalances receive much attention—those with Mexico and Japan (figure 6.2c). In the case of Mexico, the rapid and significant change in both relative prices and income growth associated with the collapse of the peso and the aftermath (1994-95) have had the effect of widening the bilateral deficit. Before that, however, the pattern of US trade with Mexico was more similar to its pattern of trade with Europe and Canada than with China. This is due in part to the integration of Mexico into the production strategy of US firms, which was greatly enhanced by the North American Free Trade Agreement (NAFTA). When Mexico produces goods for the US marketplace, it uses inputs from the United States. Hence Mexico's imports from the United States rise in tandem with its exports to the United States. On the other hand, as growth in Mexico strengthens, the US bilateral deficit should shrink as more US products are exported to satisfy domestic demand in Mexico. NAFTA negotiations have reduced the barriers facing US exports to the domestic Mexican market, so changes in the pattern of trade based on business cycles should become more apparent.

Japan is a somewhat different case, exhibiting both cyclical and structural characteristics. The difference in income growth rates has been a key factor in the dynamics of the bilateral balance, and exchange rate movements also have been important. In particular, the slow growth of the Japanese economy since 1991 has surely reduced demand for US goods and services. Yet, even though Japan has grown slowly, the US services surplus has increased steadily because US exporters of services are more competitive than the domestic providers in Japan.[5] However, structural factors likely underlie the persistently negative merchandise trade deficit,

---

5. See chapter 3 for a discussion of service-sector competitiveness, and chapter 7 for a discussion of the role of competitiveness more generally in affecting the overall trade balance.

which is difficult to explain and has been the focus of much research (Bergsten and Noland 1993, 59-97).

Bilateral Trade Negotiations, Bilateral Deficits, the Overall US Deficit, and the Question of Sustainability

Just because macroeconomic forces and comparative advantage are important does not mean that trade policies have no effect on bilateral balances. Japan, perhaps more than any other country, has been much studied for whether its trading patterns evidence policy or institutional discrimination against certain types of products. Such policies or institutions might have a particularly negative impact on US exports. The composition of the US bilateral deficit with Japan does appear peculiar, since it is concentrated in autos and, to a lesser extent, computers and electronics products, and it seems relatively unaffected by the cycle underpinning the overall deficit (figure 6.3). The National Trade Estimate Report on Foreign Trade Barriers consistently devotes more pages to Japan than to any other country.[6] The United States has initiated numerous and extensive bilateral negotiations with Japan to "open up" its markets.[7] Some evidence suggests that this persistence has paid off, in terms of relatively faster growth of US exports in the targeted sectors.[8] In more recent years, the very rapid increase in the US bilateral deficit with China has also been the object of much analysis, outrage, and negotiation.[9]

However, the question in this section is not whether bilateral trade negotiations can open up particular markets and lead to greater US exports, nor even whether such trade policy initiatives can alter the magnitude of a bilateral balance. Undoubtedly such negotiations can achieve

6. Congress established the annual National Trade Estimate Report on Foreign Trade Barriers in 1984 in order to help prioritize the administration's trade negotiations. The Office of the US Trade Representative must identify significant foreign trade barriers, dollar value of lost trade, efforts to eliminate the barriers, and US priorities to expand export markets. (See also Bayard and Elliott 1994, p. 28, box 2.1.)

7. The focus of these negotiations has included agricultural products, ranging from apples and beef to fish and wood products; manufactured goods, in the sectors of automobiles and auto parts, semiconductors, supercomputers, and telecommunications equipment as well as flat glass and amorphous materials; and the services sectors, such as construction, financial services, and insurance.

8. Council of Economic Advisers, *Economic Report of the President*, 1996, p. 246, chart 8.1.

9. Several researchers focus on the issue of how large the US-China deficit really is, particularly since the Chinese and US accounts treat trade between the United States and Hong Kong in different ways. See, for example, Feenstra et al. (1998). Negotiations have been conducted on specific sectors, such as intellectual property, as well as very broadly, in the context of Chinese accession to the World Trade Organization.

Figure 6.3 Composition of US-Japan bilateral deficit, 1980-96

billions of US dollars

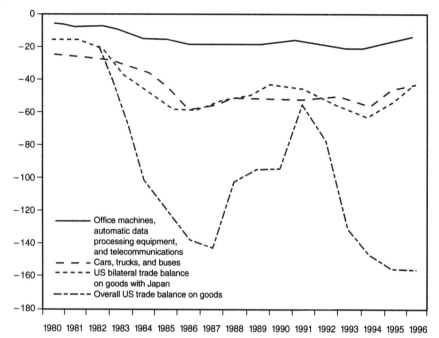

Source: Statistics Canada, *World Trade Analyzer*; US Department of Commerce, *US International Trade Goods and Services.*

those goals. The question here is, Can bilateral negotiations reduce the *overall* trade deficit and thus contribute to sustainability? To answer this, we return to the macroeconomic framework of chapter 2. A net export deficit develops when national savings are insufficient to finance domestic investment. Consequently, to affect the trade balance, bilateral trade negotiations must affect one or the other of these variables or their components. For example, a bilateral market-opening negotiation could affect external balance if it changed the national savings rate, say, by increasing business net profitability or by raising the household savings rate.

But how can an increase in the *level* of exports to a particular market affect the national savings *rate*? Figure 6.4 is a schematic of the relationships among the variables. Suppose market-access negotiations successfully raise US exports to a large trading partner (figure 6.4a), such as Japan or China.[10] If the exporting firms exhibit economies of scale, the

10. Indeed, Bergsten and Noland (1993) suggest that such efforts could cut $9 billion to $18 billion from the 1990 levels of the US bilateral deficit with Japan. The gain to the United States from China's accession to the WTO under the deal as proposed in May 1999 would be $3 billion (Rosen 1999).

Figure 6.4 Market-opening trade policy and trade balance

T0: Market-opening policy implemented
T1: Normal spending behavior resumes

A. Target market exports

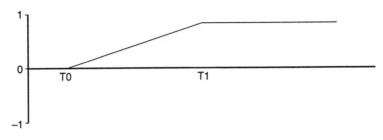

B. Business plus household savings rate

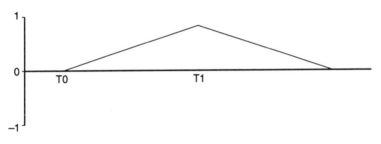

C. Overall exports and imports

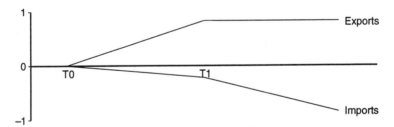

D. Overall balances

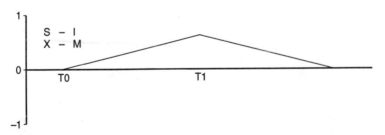

increased sales will reduce costs and contribute to increased corporate profits. If these firms hire workers who previously were unemployed and who now work and save, the increased export sales will increase household savings. If the increase in private-sector profits and workers' savings *are not spent*, the economywide savings rate will increase. Consequently, the savings-investment balance will change, and both the bilateral and the global US external balances will improve. By this logic a targeted market-opening policy could improve not only a bilateral balance but the overall balance as well.

Why, however, should firms enjoying higher sales from newly achieved access to the export market not use those profits in the same way that they use profits generated from any other increase in sales? And why should the newly hired workers be more frugal than their already working colleagues? The firms will still need to purchase inputs, some of which will be imports. In addition, they may decide to invest in new plant or technology to support the increase in sales. Hence even if business profitability might rise initially, it will ultimately return to a normal rate of profit. The newly hired workers may pay off some debts (which raises the rate of household savings), but ultimately they will return to their normal consumption path (figure 6.4b), and some of what they consume will be imported goods. Market-opening trade policies increase exports, which, if everything else remains unchanged, will increase income, and imports rise along with income. *At the end of the adjustment* to the new bilateral trade regime, exports, income, savings, investment, and imports all will be greater, but internal and external balance will have returned to their original positions (figure 6.4c,d).

Hence market-opening bilateral trade negotiations will have salutary effects on many economic variables that policymakers care about, such as exports, jobs, and income. But such policies will not narrow the trade imbalance by nearly as much as some might think, particularly after adjustment to the export gain has taken place. A simple correlation of exports and imports bears this out: Controlling for changes in US GDP growth, an increase by $1 in exports raises imports by $0.60.[11]

While "unfair" trade policies that *close* certain markets to US exports do contribute to US bilateral deficits, they are not a significant cause of the large—and particularly not of the increasing—US external deficit. This is all the more obvious given the *opening* of markets abroad through the reduction in trade barriers around the world during the 1980s and 1990s as part of the Uruguay Round of the General Agreement on Tariffs and Trade, on account of sectoral negotiations, and as a result of unilateral liberalization by some of our trading partners.

---

11. Since increased exports would raise GDP, and would raise imports, this calculation represents a lower bound on the relationship between export growth and import growth.

Multilateral Service-Sector Negotiations, the Overall US Trade Deficit, and the Question of Sustainability

Empirical analysis of the behavior of the US external balance suggests that there are systematic differences in the magnitude of the response of goods flows and services flows to changes in US and foreign income.[12] Decades of empirical work show that when US and foreign incomes rise, the tendency for the United States to spend the additional income on imports is about one and one-half to two times the tendency of other countries to spend their additional income on US exports. Therefore, if US and foreign incomes grow at the same rate, the US trade balance tends to worsen.

However, this asymmetry in responsiveness of trade to changes in income is reversed for trade in services (see table 8.2). That is, the tendency of the United States to purchase service imports is less than the tendency of foreigners to purchase US service exports when income rises. This makes sense; the United States enjoys global comparative advantage in the services sector and has a trade surplus in services.

In 1998, services constituted about one-third of US exports of goods and services and about one-sixth of US imports of goods and services; and the export share was rising faster. Over time, as the share of services in total US trade increases, the asymmetry as measured by the responsiveness of total trade to changes in income could disappear. Also over time, as other countries develop and demand more imports of services, the US surplus in services trade is likely to expand.

Why would multilateral service-sector negotiations affect the savings-investment balance differently than the bilateral market-opening negotiations highlighted in the previous section? First, as a multilateral effort, the impact on US firms and workers would be broader. As noted, service exports constituted 30 percent of US total real exports in 1998, 55 percent of corporate profits, 75 percent of US real GDP, and 80 percent of non-agricultural payroll employment. No bilateral market-opening negotiation will affect this share of US exports, or this share of the US economy. For example, one of the most hard-fought market-opening negotiations was the US-Japan agreement on autos and auto parts. In 1997 these sectors accounted for 6 percent of US total exports and less than half that as a share of real GDP. Consequently, the impact of multilateral service-sector negotiations on the US economy is simply much greater and much more broad-based. An increase in private savings (corporate and household) is more likely to accrue and be retained.

Finally, the globalization of production in the goods sector (which accounts for the fact that every dollar of exports is associated with $0.60 of

---

12. For more details on the income and relative price framework for analyzing trade, see chapter 8.

imports, controlling for US real GDP growth) is far less pervasive in services. Service establishments often do locate abroad to be close to the customer, and service-sector negotiations will facilitate this movement. But when exported from a base in the United States, services are less import intensive than goods are. Consequently, service-sector negotiations will have a disproportionate impact on exports and a less-than-proportionate impact on imports.

Trade in services therefore should be a focal point for US negotiators in the next round of trade negotiations. The Uruguay Round began the process of liberalizing trade in services but left the majority of barriers in place (Hoekman 1995; Snape and Bosworth 1996). The objective for the year 2000 negotiations is further liberalization in key service sectors (Feketekuty 1998). Greater liberalization of service-sector trade in other countries would help narrow the overall deficit, and thus would contribute to making the US current account sustainable.

Trade Deficits and US Trade Policy Reaction

The 1980s: Aggressive Unilateralism

Worsening trade deficits, particularly bilateral deficits and deficits in particular industries, often precipitate demands for protection, for the opening of foreign markets, or for any policy initiative that might increase exports and/or reduce imports in the affected industries. This is precisely what we saw in the mid-1980s, when the US current account was headed toward a deficit amounting to 3.5 percent of GDP ($185 billion). Legislation, voluntary export restraints, antidumping duties, threatened generalized import surcharges, and unilateral "results-oriented" policies all were part of the policy mix.[13]

The initial response to the widening trade deficit in 1981 was specific protection for autos and steel. The first broad legislative salvo followed in 1984 and focused on raising exports. One of the provisions of the Trade and Tariff Act of 1984 was to authorize the Office of the US Trade Representative (USTR) to initiate Section 301 trade cases itself, rather than to wait for an industry to bring a case. It was also this bill that required the USTR to produce the annual National Trade Estimates Report on Foreign Trade Barriers mentioned earlier.

Legislative attention then turned to imports. In 1985 Congress considered nearly 100 trade bills—almost four times the rate of the previous three years—that were protectionist in intent and that favored specific industries—autos, steel, machine tools, motorcycles (Bayard and Elliott

---

13. This section draws extensively from Bayard and Elliott (1994, 34-49), and the references cited therein. See also Destler (1995).

1994, 16). The same year, Senate Finance Committee Chairman Lloyd Bentsen (D-TX), House Ways and Means Committee Chairman Dan Rostenkowski (D-IL), and Representative Richard Gephardt (D-MO) introduced legislation that would have imposed a 25 percent tariff surcharge against countries with "excessive" trade surpluses.

Although the "Gephardt amendment" was (narrowly) rejected, the Omnibus Trade and Competitiveness Act of 1988 included the so-called Super 301 provision. This provision, which was authorized for 1989 and 1990, required that the president identify "priority" countries, as measured by number or pervasiveness of unfair trade practices. A program and timetable for negotiations on opening targeted sectors was required, and retaliation of some sort was a distinct possibility if negotiations failed to produce results.

The 1990s: The Same Brew?

The worsening of the US trade balance from the end of 1997 through the first quarter of 1999 rivals that of the 1980s. The merchandise trade deficit, the flash point for trade disputes, grew by $50 billion in 1998 and added another $6 billion in the first quarter of 1999 compared to the year earlier. Imports surged (as defined in table 6.1) in 28 product categories accounting for 15 percent of imports by value. The iron and steel categories accounted for 2 percent of total imports and 11 percent of the "surging" imports, so it is perhaps not surprising that this industry was first in line to demand protection.

In March 1999 the House of Representatives overwhelmingly passed legislation to put quotas on steel imports, though it was defeated in the Senate in June. Antidumping actions against steel imports were successful, and "voluntary" agreements to reduce steel imports were negotiated with some countries. Other bills in both House and Senate are being drafted to alter and strengthen the way in which existing Section 201 "safeguard" provisions can be applied to any industry facing a surge of imports. As the trade deficit widens, will the legislative agenda for 2000 come to look like that of 1985?

The legislative agenda likely will play out differently. First, $23 billion of the 1998 deterioration in the merchandise trade balance was due to a widening of the imbalances of the countries immersed in the Asian financial crises. (This figure does not include Japan and China, where the shifts were about $8 billion each for 1998.) Second, although the impact of imports on an industry are the same whether because of financial crisis or an appreciating dollar (as in 1985), industry reaction to surging imports this time has been tempered by the vibrant economic environment, with inflation, interest rates, and the unemployment rate at nearly half what they were in 1985, and profit rates nearly double.

Table 6.1 Import surges in 1998

	1998	1997	Growth rate	Share of total imports in 1997
	(millions of US dollars)		(percentage)	(percentage)
Total imports, census basis	913,828	870,671	5.0	100.0
Commercial vessels, other	77	24	220.8	0.0
Vessels, except scrap	4	2	100.0	0.0
Railway transportation equipment	2,059	1,251	64.6	0.1
Civilian aircraft	6,856	4,546	50.8	0.5
Other precious metals	3,930	2,643	48.7	0.3
Drilling and oilfield equipment	1,377	952	44.6	0.1
Cocoa beans	659	469	40.5	0.1
Laboratory testing instruments	1,649	1,288	28.0	0.1
Pharmaceutical prep	16,980	13,270	28.0	1.5
TVs, VCRs, etc.	13,361	10,546	26.7	1.2
Farming materials, livestock	766	609	25.8	0.1
Dairy products and eggs	893	711	25.6	0.0
Materials handling equipment	5,421	4,325	25.3	0.5
Excavating machinery	5,481	4,381	25.1	0.5
Engines—civilian aircraft	9,403	7,591	23.9	0.9
Shingles, wallboard	5,209	4,215	23.6	0.5
Stone, sand, cement, etc.	2,544	2,098	21.3	0.2
Iron and steel mill products	13,157	10,889	20.8	1.3
Parts—civilian aircraft	5,353	4,461	20.0	0.5
Vegetables	3,499	2,937	19.1	0.3
Furniture, household goods, etc.	9,732	8,269	17.7	0.9
Nonmonetary gold	3,603	3,072	17.3	0.4
Apparel, household goods— cotton	27,807	23,953	16.1	2.8
Motorcycles and parts	1,380	1,191	15.9	0.1
Records, tapes, and disks	1,136	982	15.7	0.1
Medicinal equipment	7,934	6,864	15.6	0.8
Iron and steel products, n.e.c.	4,112	3,560	15.5	0.4
Nonfarm tractors and parts	814	705	15.5	0.1

n.e.c. = not elsewhere classified
Note: Import surge is defined here as import growth rates at least three times greater than the average growth of imports for 1997-98.

Source: US Department of Commerce, *International Trade in Goods and Services.*

Another key difference underpinning any specific trade legislation is the stalemate on general trade policy, as evidenced by the failure of efforts to renew "fast-track" trade negotiating authority for the president after it expired in 1994. The sources of this stalemate and its effects on US trade policy and initiatives—specific and general, domestic and external—are beyond the scope of this book (see Destler 1995); suffice it to say here that the issue will be of great importance as the US economy likely slows into 2000 and the trade deficit widens further. The trajectory of the US deficit and its macroeconomic and political sustainability are discussed further in chapter 10.

Conclusion

Summary

■ Bilateral imbalances are almost an inevitable outcome of different resource endowments, tastes, levels of development, and cycles of economic activity; a zero bilateral trade balance is a rare event.

■ An examination of the behavior of US bilateral balances with countries and regions of the world supports the notion that the macroeconomic factors of differences in income growth and changes in relative prices are key drivers of many bilateral and certainly the overall trade balances. That said, some bilateral deficits are determined more by level of economic development, and a few arise from restrictions on exports from the United States.

■ Bilateral trade negotiations can open particular markets, lead to greater US exports, and reduce a bilateral deficit. But is that negotiating effort well spent? Do such bilateral approaches affect the *overall* US trade deficit? To affect the overall balance, bilateral trade policy must work through the channels of savings and investment—for example, by changing business profitability or the household savings rate. Simply altering the level of exports into a particular market will do relatively little to change these savings rates; consequently, bilateral trade efforts generally will not significantly narrow the overall trade gap.

■ Multilateral and broad-based initiatives to liberalize trade in services are more likely to improve the overall deficit. The United States has global comparative advantage in services, and services remain highly protected abroad. As economies grow, the share of services in consumption increases; with liberalization, their share in US exports would increase too. Statistical analysis suggests that, as income rises in foreign economies, they consume a relatively higher fraction of US exports of services than of US exports of goods. The sustainability of the

US external deficit would be enhanced by a growing share of services in US trade.

Policy Discussion

■ A continually growing US external deficit will raise the volume of calls for protection. Sector-specific and bilaterally focused trade protection measures will clutter the domestic legislative agenda and poison the international negotiating waters. Explicit advocacy of a new multilateral round of fixed duration and with key sectors foremost on the agenda would create the greatest impetus for meaningful liberalization and the greatest likelihood of changing the overall trade balance.

■ US negotiators should push beyond the standstill of the GATS in the Uruguay Round and offer more rapid access to markets in key sectors attractive to the developing countries (e.g., textiles, apparel, and agriculture) in return for meaningful service-sector liberalization. Pursuit of market-opening commitments in the service sector should also be a priority in regional negotiations.

7

Is There a Good Measure of Competitiveness?

The trade deficit may have its limitations as a statistic, but it is our best measure of America's international competitiveness. . . . Our deficit can be financed only by more debt or the selling of assets. This is a strange definition of economic health.

—Jeff Faux, President of the Economic Policy Institute, letter to the editor,
New York Times (26 November 1997)

The United States is far and away the most competitive large country.

—Executive Summary, World Economic Forum,
Global Competitiveness Report (1998)

[T]he United States will not keep its competitive edge as a nation unless long-term vulnerabilities in saving, investment, research, and education are overcome.

—John Yochelson, "Can the U.S. Compete? A Ten-Year Outlook,"
Chief Executive (June 1997)

By many measures, the United States is the world leader. Most technological innovations originate in US universities and businesses. Many US exporters are the world's most cost-efficient producers. US financial institutions make financial capital work more efficiently to meet business needs around the globe. The United States tops the World Economic Forum's measure of international competitiveness (the "Davos index").

Yet the external deficit continues to widen. Why does the competitiveness of universities, exporters, financial institutions, and other elements of the US economy not translate into a positive trade balance? Is external balance a good measure of the competitiveness of a nation? Are there better measures?

There are several approaches to measuring national competitiveness. One is to link price competitiveness, a microeconomic concept, with external balance, a macroeconomic concept. The prices of exports and imports that drive trade flows and thus external balance are determined in part by the costs and strategies of individual businesses, for which microeconomic concepts of price competitiveness are crucial. But macroeconomic factors such as exchange rates, which an individual firm does not control, also affect a firm's price competitiveness. Together firms' microeconomic decisions and broader macroeconomic factors affect the price competitiveness of exporters and import-competing firms, and price competitiveness is one force driving trade flows and external balance.

Price competitiveness is not the only determinant of external balance, however. The external deficit represents the collective actions of individual consumers, businesses, and government. The balance is determined by the difference between aggregate domestic production and aggregate domestic spending. When a country spends more than it produces, it will have a deficit even if in price terms its workers and producers are world-class competitors.

Moreover, prices measure competitiveness only at a given point in time. Long-term competitiveness is founded on the quality of resources firms use to produce goods and services as well as on the decisions made by households, businesses, and government to spend and save. The efficiency with which the financial markets transform savings into investment, the pace and uptake of technological innovations, the ability of workers to adjust to changing skills demanded in the workplace, and the quality of the political and policymaking processes all affect a country's long-term ability to produce and compete in the international marketplace.

Finally, purchasing power is another indicator of competitiveness. The "terms of trade" for the United States—the price of exports compared to US imports—measures the purchasing power of US exports. The more highly valued products should command relatively higher prices. So do rises in terms of trade signal improved competitiveness?

As we shall see, these different measures of competitiveness can move in opposite directions, with some suggesting an improvement in competitiveness while others suggest a deterioration. The bottom line, however, is that superior relative price competitiveness plays out in terms of higher global market share, and relative prices and market shares are better measures of competitiveness than is the trade deficit.

Determinants of Relative Prices and Implications for Competitiveness

External balance is a macroeconomic concept that rests uncomfortably on the microeconomic foundation of relative prices. As discussed in chapter

2, external balance can be described in two equivalent ways: as the difference between production and consumption by all members of the economy, or as the difference between exports and imports. What are the economic incentives that drive the firm to choose what to produce in the
national economy and how much to sell abroad? How do consumers decide what to buy, and whether to buy domestic or imported goods?

The key factor in such decisions is the relative price of similar products
that compete with each other and that can be purchased at home or abroad.
For example, a US firm selling a product in the United States competes
with other domestic producers' products as well as with imported products. A US exporter's goods and services compete with similar products
sold by domestic firms in the destination market as well as with those
produced by other firms in third countries. Hence what matters for production and demand decisions is the *relative price* of the good or service.
But what the firm controls, at least in part, is its own *absolute price*.

What determines the absolute price, and then the more important relative price, of a good or service? Very simply, a product's price is determined by costs of production and the margin or markup that the firm adds
for profit. In the case of internationally traded products, the exchange rate,
which translates the price quoted by the firm into the buyer's currency, is
also a critical component of the relative price. Using this simple pricing
structure, we can point out some key sources of international price competitiveness that will affect the external balance. The relative price of US
products to competing foreign products is just the ratio of the US price to
the foreign price; its components are the relative costs, the relative markups, and the exchange rate of the foreign currency to US dollars.

These ratios illustrate that what firms control most directly as part of a
business strategy (the markup or profit margin) is only one element of the
relative price and thus of how much a firm will sell. The firm does not
control many aspects of costs, nor does the firm control the exchange rate.
In short, many factors outside the firm's control will affect relative prices,
sales, production, and demand. They will also affect the relative shares of
demand satisfied by domestic products and by imports, which in turn directly affects the external balance.

Table 7.1 illustrates a hypothetical example that focuses only on how
the exchange rate can affect the relative price. A US product is sold for
2,750 yen in Japan (line 1). This absolute price is determined by a cost of
production in the United States of $25, a profit margin of 10 percent (1.10),
and an exchange rate of 100 yen to the dollar. This US product competes
with a Japanese product priced at 3,300 yen (line 2), which is composed of
a cost of production in Japan of 3,000 yen and a profit margin of 10 percent (1.10). At the exchange rate of 100 yen per dollar, the US product is
competitively priced in Japan; that is, its price in Japan is much lower than
its domestically produced substitute. In fact, the relative price of the US
product is 20 percent lower than the Japanese product. In a product class

Table 7.1 Price, profit margins, and exchange rates

$$[P_{US}/P_{FJ}] = [V_{US}/V_{FJ}] * [C_{US}/C_{FJ}] * [E_{FX\$}]$$

P = Price   US = United States
V = Profit margin   F = Foreign country
C = Costs   FX = Foreign currency
E = Exchange rate (foreign/$)

	Price		Cost of production	Margin		Exchange rate	Line
Initial exchange rate = 100 yen/$							
US product	2,750 yen	=	25 $ ×	1.10	×	100 yen/$	1
Japanese product	3,300 yen	=	3,000 yen ×	1.10	×	1 yen/yen	2
New exchange rate = 125 yen/$							
US product	3,438 yen	=	25 $ ×	1.10	×	125 yen/$	3
Japanese product	3,300 yen	=	3,000 yen ×	1.10	×	1 yen/yen	4
If							
US firm meets the Japanese price	3,300 yen	=	25 $ ×	1.056	×	125 yen/$	5
US firm maintains relative price advantage	2,750 yen	=	25 $ ×	0.88	×	125 yen/$	6

characterized by intra-industry trade (as discussed in chapter 3), the US producer probably will not take over the whole market despite this relative price advantage, but it is likely to export its product to Japan.[1]

What if the yen depreciates to 125 yen per dollar? At this exchange rate, with all other elements of the model unchanged, the yen price of the US product is 3,438 yen (line 3). The US producer's cost structure in the United States has not changed, but the US product is now priced uncompetitively in the Japanese market, in absolute as well as in relative terms.

The US producer can match the Japanese price by reducing its profit margin from 10 percent to 5.6 percent (line 5). But if it wants to maintain its previous *relative* price advantage of 20 percent (2,750 yen versus 3,300 yen), and thus retain the market share it had prior to the exchange rate change, it would have to reduce its profit margin to 0.88—that is, take a loss of 12 percent on each sale (line 6). In the face of this exchange rate change, if the US firm does not change its pricing behavior, it will lose market share and will export less. With a change in its margins, it could still make some sales, although fewer, which implies fewer exports, and at a loss to profit per unit sold. The lower profitability could have implications for stock-market valuation, investment, future growth, and so on. Moreover, the exchange rate can move beyond the point at which profit margins can absorb the currency fluctuations; clearly, the thinner the margins initially, the less room there is to cut them any thinner in the face of exchange rate fluctuations. The firm must decide whether to abandon the market (reducing exports to zero), or to stay in and, along with working hard to reduce costs and convincing stockholders that it makes sense to absorb currency fluctuations into profits, hope that the yen will appreciate back to its previous level.[2]

The Key Role of Labor Costs and Quality

Labor costs account for a large share of the costs of production and thus of the absolute price of a product.[3] Understanding how labor costs change over time is crucial for explaining relative price competitiveness. There are two main dimensions to labor costs—direct costs and quality. Direct costs

---

1. Moreover, at this exchange rate, the United States is the lower-cost producer (yen costs are 3,000 yen and the US producer's cost in yen terms is 2,500 yen), so there are global efficiencies in resource utilization generated by US production and exports.

2. Hedging the revenue streams in yen using forward exchange rate contracts would complicate the model without fundamentally changing the result.

3. When imported intermediate goods are used as inputs in the production process, exchange rates play an enhanced role. Evidence suggests that imported intermediates are playing an increasingly important role in the production process.

of labor, such as wage and nonwage compensation, can change over relatively short periods. Quality of labor—that is, productivity, skills, creativity, and flexibility—changes more slowly, and over longer time spans. In evaluating US competitiveness, we might wish to know how US labor compares to labor in other countries in terms of the relatively simple dimension of direct costs as well as the more complex dimension of productivity-adjusted cost.

The first way to gauge what is happening to labor costs is to compare how they have changed in the United States with how they have changed in other countries—each in its own national currency. As figure 7.1a shows, US labor compensation nearly doubled between 1980 and 1997 (the index number rose from 100 to almost 200). Over the same period, German labor costs initially rose somewhat less slowly than US labor costs and then around 1990 started to rise a bit more quickly than US labor costs. Japan shows a similar pattern, although labor compensation has been rising at nearly the same rate as in the United States over the years. In comparison, labor compensation in South Korea has been rising at a much higher rate than US compensation over the whole period (note the different scale on the right axis of figure 7.1a), with the rate of increase accelerating from 1987 to 1996.[4]

Growth in labor compensation in national currencies provides only a partial picture of how labor costs might affect international price competitiveness. A first adjustment must account for differences between the United States and other countries in growth in labor productivity. That is, compensation may be rising faster in another country than in the United States, but if the workers' productivity is rising even faster, then the real cost of labor in terms of what the producer is using it to "create" is falling.

On this productivity-adjusted basis (but still in national currencies), figure 7.1b shows that US unit labor costs trended upward between 1980 and 1992, with periods of faster and slower growth coinciding generally with inflation, output, and productivity conditions. Since 1992, however, US unit labor costs have fallen, because the inflation rate generally has decreased (reducing upward momentum in wage costs) and growth in both output and productivity have been quite robust. German unit labor costs in deutsche marks have risen much faster than those of the United States in dollars, and have evidenced a very different cyclical pattern. Between 1980 and 1997, German unit labor costs rose about 20 percent more than

---

4. These figures compare changes in labor costs over time and cannot be used to compare labor cost *levels*. For some business decisions, such as where to site a new labor-intensive plant, the level of labor costs, productivity-adjusted and in a common currency, is relevant. However, it is quite difficult to compare labor cost levels across countries. Hooper and Vrankovich (1997) present a detailed and data-intensive methodology to compare the level of productivity-adjusted labor costs in a common currency for the G-3. However, to analyze how competitiveness in the international context is changing over time, changes in labor costs (as discussed and presented in the text and figures) are more relevant.

Figure 7.1 Comparative labor costs

A. Labor compensation in national currency relative to US dollar, 1980-97

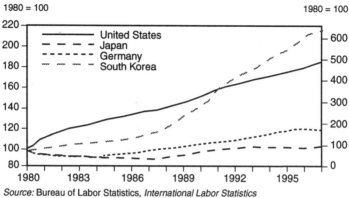

Source: Bureau of Labor Statistics, *International Labor Statistics*
<ftp://ftp.bls.gov/pub/special.requests/ForeignLabor/supptab.txt>.

B. Unit labor cost in national currency relative to the United States, 1980-97

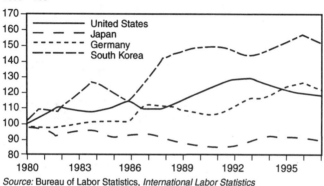

Source: Bureau of Labor Statistics, *International Labor Statistics*
<http://stats.bls.gov/news/release.prod4.t09.htm>.

C. Unit labor cost in PPP base relative to the United States, 1980-98

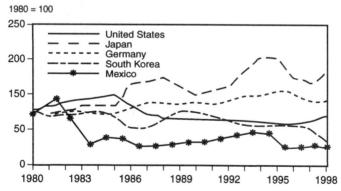

Source: Organization for Economic Cooperation and Development, *OECD Economic Outlook.*
Note: The ratios shown for the other countries are calculated as the country index relative
to the US index. Thus, for example, in the first figure an index value of 100 for another country
means that that country's compensation in its national currency units is rising at the same rate
as US compensation in dollars.

did US unit labor costs (the relative unit labor cost index for Germany stands at about 120 in 1997). By contrast, unit labor costs in Japan have risen more slowly than in the United States (the relative unit labor cost index value for Japan is below 100 throughout the period). Finally, South Korean unit labor costs have risen much more rapidly than in the United States; about one-half of the gap between the levels of US and South Korean unit labor costs was eroded in less than 20 years.

These unit labor cost ratios measure costs in national currencies. Calculating relative price competitiveness in global markets requires a common currency benchmark. We could simply use market exchange rates to calculate compensation on the basis of a common currency (say, the dollar), but market exchange rates can fluctuate for reasons that have nothing to do with external balance or productivity growth. Moreover, firms are not likely to use this measure when comparing labor costs across countries, because they are selling to destinations other than the United States. Using exchange rates measured on the basis of purchasing power parities (PPPs) yields a more realistic international comparison of unit labor costs instead of simply a comparison in dollar terms. As shown in figure 7.1c, this international benchmark reveals a picture very different from the other two, in which exchange rates are not involved.

On a PPP-adjusted basis, unit labor cost in the United States rose during the phase of dollar appreciation through 1985, but then started a downward trend that only recently appears to have reversed. On a PPP-adjusted basis, US unit labor costs have returned to about the level they were in 1980 instead of being about 20 percent higher (compare the index value for the United States in figures 7.1b and 7.1c in 1997). The behavior for comparator countries is quite different when compared in national currency and on a PPP basis.

Japanese PPP-adjusted unit labor costs have risen some 70 percent relative to US costs, although the relative rate of growth has been quite volatile. This contrasts with the relative decline in yen terms. German PPP-adjusted unit labor costs have risen some 20 percent more than US costs, about what occurred in deutsche mark terms. South Korean and Mexican PPP-adjusted unit labor costs, in contrast, have fallen relative to those in the United States; the gap between the levels of unit labor costs quoted in a common currency has widened by some 50 percent since 1980; in national currency terms, just the opposite was taking place, at least in South Korea.

In summary, in order to gauge how the "competitiveness" of US labor is changing, we need to know not just the compensation figures, but also how productive labor is. When judging labor costs in the international arena, an adjustment for currency fluctuations is necessary. It is clear from the comparisons of unit labor costs on a national versus an international basis that the exchange rate adjustment can sometimes outweigh other adjustments in determining relative labor cost competitiveness. Since labor

Table 7.2 Average annual growth of exports and imports (percentage)

	1973-79	1980-85	1986-90	1991-96	1997-98
Real exports	5.2	-1.9	12.8	8.9	2.5
Real imports	4.0	15.0	3.5	11.2	11.9

Source: IMF, International Financial Statistics.

is a key component of business costs, it is clear that macroeconomic policies that determine exchange rates can and do have a material impact on relative price competitiveness.

Linking Relative Price Competitiveness to the Trade Balance

One of the epigraphs at the beginning of this chapter indicates that some people measure the international competitiveness of the United States by the trade balance. In the previous section we saw how competitiveness can be measured by relative prices, which constitute one determinant of the trade balance. How are these two measures—trade balance and relative prices—linked? Do they tell the same story about international competitiveness? Two key factors that link relative prices and the trade balance are movements in the exchange value of the dollar and movements in income growth.

When the exchange value of the dollar moves dramatically, changes in the relative prices of exports and imports can be the prime mover of the flows of imports and exports that determine the US external balance. This was illustrated most clearly in the 1980s, when the dollar appreciated some 50 percent between 1981 and early 1985 and then depreciated nearly the same amount in 1989. As the dollar appreciated during the first half of the 1980s, the relative prices of exports rose and real exports fell at an average annual rate of 1.9 percent (table 7.2). During that period, the relative prices of imports fell and imports grew at an average annual rate of 15 percent. The external balance worsened substantially.

Conversely, as the dollar depreciated during the latter half of the 1980s, export flows boomed, with average annual growth into the double digits at 12.8 percent, and import growth slowed to 3.5 percent. It was a puzzle at the time as to why demand for imports did not slow even more. On examination, it appears that foreign producers chose to contract profit margins to absorb the appreciation of their currencies, just as in the case of the hypothetical example above.[5] The period of the appreciating dollar was

---

5. Growth in incomes at home and abroad also had a key role in determining the dynamics of the US external balance. This example highlights the effects of changes in exchange rates and profit margins. For more on the puzzling behavior of the US external balances during this period, see Mann (1986), Hooper and Mann (1987), Cline (1989), and Krugman (1991).

Figure 7.2 US relative export prices and global market share, 1981-97

1995 = 100   percentage

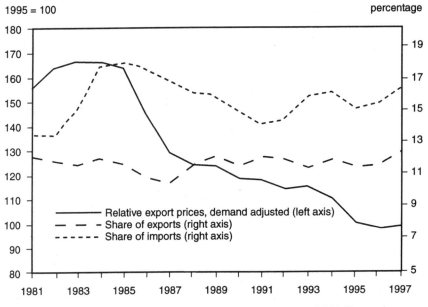

Source: Organization for Economic Cooperation and Development, *OECD Economic Outlook* (December 1997).

associated with improved terms of trade (rising export prices relative to import prices) but a deterioration in the trade balance, with exports falling and imports rising.

A second way to use trade flows instead of relative prices to measure international competitiveness is to examine the share of US exports and imports in global exports and imports. The share of global trade implicitly incorporates both price competitiveness and differentials in GDP growth.[6] For example, suppose relative prices remain unchanged, but a country has strong domestic demand during a period when the rest of the world is in recession. That country would tend to absorb a greater share of world imports than if the rest of the world also was growing strongly. Conversely, if all parts of the world were growing at about the same rate, but the relative price of US exports compared to their competitors' prices was falling, US exports would tend to capture a greater share of the global market.

These measures of competitiveness—demand-adjusted relative prices and global market shares—yield a mixed picture for the United States (figure 7.2). On the one hand, the demand-adjusted relative price of US exports has been falling since 1985. This is rather remarkable given the

---

6. For a discussion of the construction method, see Durand, Madaschi, and Terribile (1998).

development of new suppliers worldwide, the appreciation of the dollar from 1996 on, and the slow growth in the major markets of Mexico and Japan. In the face of global competition for markets, US exporters have become highly productive and acutely price conscious. The decline in relative export prices has kept US exporters' global market share from eroding. On the other hand, the US market is now absorbing a greater share of imports from around the globe than at any other time since the mid-1980s. Moreover, the US share of the world's imports is much higher than the US share in the world's export market, which is consistent with the large US external deficit. So is the United States "uncompetitive" because it has a trade deficit, or is it "supercompetitive" because its global market share of exports is higher than it has been at any time in the past 20 years?

What the data show us is that, on the basis of relative prices, the United States is globally competitive, but other factors besides relative prices drive the external balance—specifically, income growth rates. When the US grows faster than its trading partners and consumes more than it produces, these macro factors can outweigh internationally competitive relative prices and business strategies, and a trade deficit results. Consequently, a country's competitiveness is better measured by relative price competitiveness, particularly the labor cost component. Changes in global market share will reflect this type of competitiveness, but the trade balance may not.

Terms of Trade, Purchasing Power, and Competitiveness

Improved competitiveness should raise a nation's standard of living. The terms of trade measure the price of exports compared to imports. If the price of the products a country sells on international markets rises relative to the price of the products it buys on international markets, then the terms of trade move to favor the exporting country. If the rest of the world is willing to pay a high price for what the United States produces, then does this not mean that the US products are highly desired on world markets? It certainly means that US exports can purchase more imports, and this implies that US resources and income can support a higher standard of living. That is, the United States need give up fewer resources (as embodied in exports) to exchange for the imports that are used to satisfy domestic demand.

An improvement in the terms of trade thus is associated with a higher standard of living. However, higher export prices will reduce foreign sales, and lower import prices will raise imports. Thus an improvement in the terms of trade can be associated with a rising trade deficit (figure 7.3). As the trade deficit becomes unsustainable (see chapter 10), the terms of trade become a poor measure of competitiveness, since rises in terms of trade sow the seeds of the depreciation of the exchange value of the dol-

Figure 7.3 Terms of trade and balance of trade, 1980-98

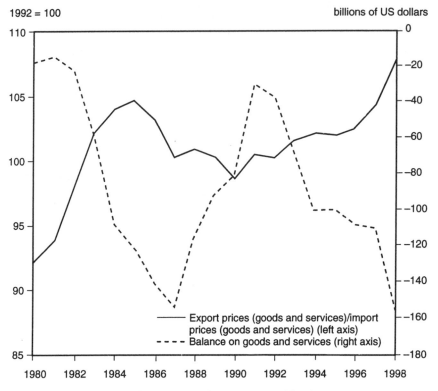

Sources: US Department of Commerce, *National Income and Product Accounts;
International Transactions Tables.*

lar (which translates into a deterioration in the terms of trade) necessary
to close the trade deficit. Consequently the terms of trade is not a good
measure of competitiveness.

Competitiveness through Globalization:
The Ownership-Based Supplement

An entirely different method of measuring US international competitiveness focuses on multinational businesses and their links through trade
and direct investment. More than one-third of sales of goods and services
by US firms in foreign markets and by foreign firms in the US market
occur through multinationals. Nearly 40 percent of US exports and about
30 percent of imports are between parent corporations and affiliates. By
balance of payments conventions, the sales of goods and services by affil-

iates in a country to customers there are not recorded in the trade statistics, since these transactions occur within a country, not across a border (see US Department of Commerce, *Survey of Current Business,* October 1997). (The profits earned on these transactions do enter the current account as a component of investment income.)

Should affiliate sales be linked to the external accounts? If they were, what might be the consequences for recorded trade flows, the external balance, and concepts of competitiveness? There are three models for how affiliate sales might affect cross-border trade:[7] Affiliate sales can substitute for cross-border exports, the two can be complementary, or affiliate sales may be impossible without a physical presence in the destination market.

Researchers have investigated the impact of corporate relationships on recorded trade to determine whether the substitution model or the complements model appears to better explain the relationship between trade and affiliate sales. They found that, in general, cross-border trade and direct investment are positively related, and hence they reject the model in which trade and affiliate sales are substitutes (Lipsey 1991; Graham and Krugman 1991).

Because trade flows and affiliate sales are tightly linked, some argue that a better measure of external relations and of external balance would be to add sales by affiliates to cross-border sales. The "total sales" approach was proposed by DeAnne Julius and subsequently refined by the National Academy of Sciences as well as the OECD. In some respects these methods present, in an aggregate way that is consistent with macroeconomic accounting, how corporations account for their own international relationships.

The US Department of Commerce's Bureau of Economic Analysis (BEA) evaluated various approaches to accounting for international relationships and developed a supplemental account to the standard balance of payments (see US Department of Commerce, *Survey of Current Business,* October 1995). This supplemental account retains the distinction between cross-border trade and trade that occurs between suppliers, affiliates, and customers within the destination market. It is therefore consistent with historical balance-of-payments data, with other countries' balance-of-payments data, and with national income and product accounts conventions. The BEA supplement presents the gross value of sales by affiliates and also disaggregates those data into inputs from the parents' own market, inputs from foreign markets, and intracompany sales in the parents' own market. To arrive at the so-called ownership-based concept of the balance of trade, the BEA sums the value of trade in goods and services with net receipts resulting from sales by affiliates.

---

7. Parallel analysis holds for both imports and exports. Most of the example here focuses on exports, because evidence from US data suggests that the export relationships are more important than the import relationships.

Figure 7.4   US external balances: Standard and ownership based, 1980-98

billions of US dollars

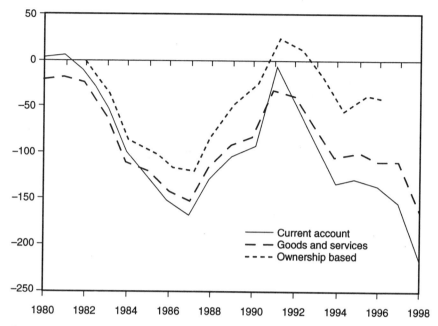

Sources: US Department of Commerce, *International Transactions Tables,·*Historical Data; *Survey of Current Business* (October 1995); *An Ownership-Based Disaggregation of the US Current Account, 1982-93.*

Figure 7.4 compares three measures of external balance: the current account, the goods and services trade balance, and the ownership-based concept. The general behavior over time of the ownership-based measure of the trade balance looks quite similar to the cross-border measures of the trade balance, although it appears that the new concept adds an increasingly positive wedge to the standard measures. This wedge reflects the positive balance in direct investment abroad and, apparently, the ability of US firms to effectively and efficiently combine US management and other assets with foreign inputs to create much greater value in markets abroad than the reverse combination of foreign management and US resources create in the United States.[8] This wedge was large enough in 1991 and 1992 to make the ownership-based measure of external balance positive, whereas the standard measures were negative. Moreover, the

8. This assessment of the comparative advantage of US management skills was first proposed in Kravis and Lipsey (1988).

wedge seems to be widening, particularly in recent years, pointing to an increasingly important competitive edge enjoyed by US firms in their relationships abroad.

The contribution to the US economy by net sales of affiliates abroad is large—$67 billion in 1996. Although these net receipts do not represent a cross-border flow of goods or capital, they do indicate the importance of international integration of production and distribution for US corporate fitness and dynamism (see chapter 3), and they may be part of the reason why productivity growth has increased (see chapter 5). Because of the benefits that come from such global integration, US policy should facilitate and promote further international integration.

The Underpinnings of Long-Term Competitiveness

A price is a summary statistic of contemporaneous inputs, macroeconomic factors, and business decisions. Prices may incorporate information on current competitiveness, but they measure only incompletely the underpinnings of competitiveness in the long term. Similarly, the external balance, however measured, summarizes the macroeconomic state of a country. The preparedness of labor for future jobs, innovation and the development of new technologies, and efficiency and management of financial resources are all important for long-term competitiveness, and these do not show up in the external balance measured at a point in time. Even if the United States is internationally competitive by many measures now, is it preparing adequately for competitiveness in the future?

Is US Labor Prepared for the Future?

Labor's preparation for the future includes, among other things, general education, skill training, flexibility, and creativity to respond to changes in the employment situation. There is no science that describes what is a "good worker." By some indicators, the United States is preparing itself well. The entry rate and completion rate for university education and the percentage of GDP devoted to education are among the highest in the OECD membership. The total student-teacher contact time in public lower secondary education exceeds the OECD average (but still is not much higher than that of several emerging-market nations). The United States has the highest percentage of computer use on a daily basis by high-school students (OECD 1998c, 15, 17, 30, and 306).

By other measures, however, US students currently in school do not fare well on the international scale, and some current workers are not prepared for the changing demands of the workplace. The percentage of students graduating from secondary school is lower than the OECD average, ranking with some countries in the emerging markets. Despite having completed secondary education, more than half of US adults (as of 1994-95) performed below the level consistent with "coping with the literacy requirements of everyday life (level 3 of the International Adult Literacy Survey)." In other OECD countries, the proportion of the population attaining secondary education was lower, but literacy rates were higher. The performance of US eighth-grade students on a standardized math test was well below the OECD average, although the performance of fourth graders met the OECD average (OECD 1998c, 22, 24, 27, 32, and 51). The United States ranked 36th among the 53 countries surveyed by the World Economic Forum for effectiveness of math and science education.[9]

Of even greater concern is the gap in educational attainment within the United States. Among OECD member countries, the United States has the greatest difference in mean score on a standardized literacy test between those with tertiary educational attainment and those with less than secondary educational attainment. The United States has the widest gap in student performance between the fourth and eighth grades in math achievement. Once out in the workforce, additional training on the job or after hours in the United States is undertaken more by those who need it less, that is, workers who are already at the upper end of the spectrum of educational attainment. Because of the gap in educational attainment, many workers are not contributing as much as they could to the short-term growth and the long-term potential of the United States. More important for these individuals, the gap is reflected in a widening disparity of income and opportunity.

Technology as the Foundation for Long-Run Competitiveness

With respect to innovation and the foundation for new technologies, the United States presents a mixed picture. By some standard measures, such as patent filings per employee, the United States ranks 21st among the 52 countries surveyed on this measure by the World Economic Forum; by an alternative measure of patents from the OECD, the United States has been surpassed by Switzerland, Australia, Sweden, Germany, and Finland. In terms of R&D as a share of GDP, the United States is outranked by Sweden, Japan, and Switzerland. However, in terms of the number of research-

---

9. The World Economic Forum is a nongovernmental organization incorporated as a foundation in 1971. The core community of the World Economic Forum is the 1,000 foremost global companies. Among its publications is the annual *Global Competitiveness Report*, which analyzes and ranks 53 countries according to a unique blend of data and information taken from a worldwide survey of corporate executives.

ers per person in the labor force, the United States is outranked only by Japan; and the United States has far and away the highest share of its researchers in the business sector. The United States has more computers per person than any other country, and the most computing power.[10]

The United States ranked highest in a management survey of 52 countries of whether the country's companies "pioneer new products and processes" and was described as the "world leader in technology." The highest ranking for commercialization of research and adoption of new technology paints a picture of a dynamic, technologically sophisticated business sector.[11]

With respect to financing innovative enterprises through venture capital, the United States stands head and shoulders above the competition. Among the countries surveyed for the World Economic Forum, the United States ranks first in the supply of venture capital and in the role of stock markets as a source of new capital, and it is second only to the United Kingdom in the sophistication of financial markets. Venture activity, measured as value of investments, was more than twice that of all of Europe in 1995, although by 1997 Europe was nearly on a par with the United States. According to the OECD, in terms of share of venture investments in GDP and seed capital as a share of total venture investment, the US venture industry's figures were nearly three times the European average and were greater by far than those of any individual European country.[12]

Measuring National Competitiveness

Measures of national competitiveness can combine a number of elements, such as the competitiveness of factors of production (such as labor), firms' business strategies (such as management and profit margin decisions), a country's institutions, and the country as a site for doing business (weighing features ranging from efficiency of taxation to predilection for corruption). The "Davos index" of international competitiveness generated by the World Economic Forum is an example of such a broad measure. The Davos index combines eight factors: openness, government, finance, infrastructure, technology, management, labor, and institutions. Each factor is an index created from subindexes composed of both quantitative and survey data. Quantitative data receive higher weight in the factor-indexes for openness, government, finance, and labor characteristics. Survey data

---

10. For patents per employee, see World Economic Forum (1998, table 5.19), and OECD (1998c, 211); for R&D indicators, see World Economic Forum (1998, table 5.15), and OECD (1998c, 210).

11. For the management survey, see World Economic Forum (1998, tables 3.06, 5.01).

12. For discussions of venture capital and financial markets, see World Economic Forum (1998, tables 3.07, 3.01); OECD (1998c, 75, table 4.2; 204, table 10.2).

receive higher weighting in the categories of infrastructure, technology, management quality, and institutions.[13]

The Davos index is a simple ranking; in this sense its value has no economic meaning either in terms of the level or of changes in competitiveness. However, using the information from the rankings of the whole set of 53 countries along with rankings of selected subindexes yields robust relationships between the rankings and issues of immediate policy relevance. For example, higher ranking in the index is correlated with faster growth in GDP per capita and with an increase in the real income of the poor (Warner 1998a, 30-37).

Conclusion

Summary

- External balance is a macroeconomic concept that rests uncomfortably on the microeconomic foundation of relative prices. Relative prices are composed of factors that the firm can control, such as profit margins, and factors that it does not control, such as exchange rates.

- By several measures of relative prices and in terms of performance in global markets, US firms are world class. Consequently, the external deficit, which some suggest indicates the "uncompetitiveness" of the US economy, is more an outcome of macroeconomic factors, such as the production-expenditure imbalance in the United States, the differences in growth rates between the United States and its trading partners, and the exchange value of the dollar.

- The preparedness of labor for future jobs, innovation and the development of new technologies, and efficiency and management of financial resources are all important elements of long-term competitiveness. While the United States is internationally competitive by many measures now, in some respects it is not preparing adequately for the future.

- Among current and future workers, many are not being adequately prepared for the jobs of the future. At least as important is the gap in performance and the widening disparity of income that comes with differences in educational attainment.

- The United States ranks very high in technological preparedness for future growth. Its companies are the most innovative, there is more financing available for new ideas, and researchers quickly commercialize their new ideas. However, by some more traditional measures

---

13. For a discussion of the methodology, see Warner (1998b, 78-80).

of future technological prowess, such as patent filings and R&D spending, the United States has lost its lead.

Policy Discussion

■ Although the trade deficit is not a good measure of international competitiveness, it does reflect imbalances and can undermine competitiveness. Policy should address these imbalances from two macroeconomic fronts. First, savings-investment imbalances in the United States need to be rectified, with particular attention paid to household savings (for more detail, see chapters 2 and 8). Second, exchange rate misalignments such as that of the 1980s should be avoided. While the dollar has appreciated since the mid-1990s, the increase is much less than that in the 1980s, and the cause is due more to crises abroad than to a mismatch of macroeconomic policies at home. Finally, while a stable and rational mix of domestic macroeconomic policy is necessary, it is not sufficient; macroeconomic imbalances in other countries must be avoided as well.

■ Over the longer term, labor force preparation and performance are critical. The United States will not be able to continue to increase its standard of living unless its workers are world class. Both future workers who are in school and current workers who are on the job deserve the best preparation and ongoing training. The evidence suggests that the needs are not being met. A partnership between the public sector, the business sector, the academic sector, the labor movement and the individual complemented by financial aid, career guidance, and personal commitment are needed to meet the challenge.

■ Technological innovation has played a critical role in the continued superior performance of the US economy. While the secret ingredient to promoting technological innovation is not known, sufficient spending on R&D and a financial market that can assess prospects and provide capital to risk-takers appear to be key elements.

■ The globalization of production and distribution by US firms and their affiliates is adding an additional wedge of value to the US economy that represents the competitive ability of US firms to combine resources and markets across the globe. Restricting firms' strategies toward international investment—through either domestic or foreign policies—will harm long-term US competitiveness.

IV

Are the Imbalances Sustainable?

8

Is the United States "Living beyond Its Means" or an "Oasis of Prosperity"?

The current prosperity . . . has a precarious foundation. It is based to a very large extent on borrowing—both from America's own future and from the rest of the world.

—C. Fred Bergsten, *America in the World Economy: A Strategy for the 1990s* (1988)

The fact that the U.S. remains an oasis of prosperity assures continued deterioration in its trade deficit, as imports grow amid weak foreign demand.

—James C. Cooper and Kathleen Madigan, *Business Week* (8 February 8, 1999)

For nearly 20 years, the real goods and services trade balance of the United States has been in deficit. Such a persistent external deficit suggests to some that as a nation we spend more than we earn, continually borrowing to maintain an illusion of prosperity. Yet a corporation borrows to build a larger plant to reap future profits, and a student goes into debt to finance an education that will provide entry to a higher-paying job after graduation. Hence borrowing per se does not indicate profligate behavior.

Moreover, even though the trade balance has been consistently negative, when it narrowed nearly to balance (1991-92), the United States was in recession, and when it widened dramatically (last half of the 1990s), the United States experienced unprecedented growth (see figure 4.1).

How should we distinguish between the causes and consequences of the cyclical component of the deficit as compared to the causes and con-

Figure 8.1 Components of US external balance: Trade balance, net investment income, and current account, 1970-98

billions of US dollars

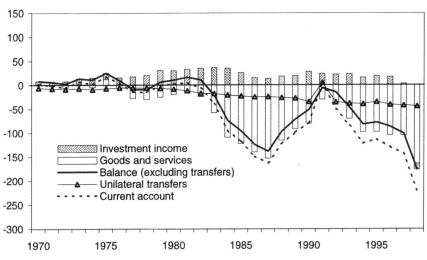

Source: US Department of Commerce, *International Transactions Tables.*

sequences of the persistent component of the deficit? There is a point at which borrowing (the counterpart of the trade deficit), even for good reasons, becomes too much. Has the United States reached that point? Specifically, in 1997 the net investment service account on the negative net international investment position turned from positive to negative, and the net payments are becoming ever larger (figure 8.1). How are these questions related to the sustainability of the deficit?

Chapter 2 outlined an approach to analyzing the external balance that focused on the domestic economy: external balance is the excess of domestic expenditure over domestic production or, expressed equivalently, domestic investment over national savings. When investment exceeds national savings, the remainder is financed by foreign savings. Similarly, if a nation wants to spend more than it earns, foreigners must be willing to accept its domestic assets in exchange for goods and services. The focus in chapter 2 on the behavior of domestic actors in the economy may have implied that foreigners respond passively to the demands of our national accounts—lending or not lending regardless of their own preferences.

This chapter offers a different, but related, perspective on the US external balance, this time with an explicit and dynamic role for foreign firms, consumers, and investors. By focusing on the forces that drive export and import *flows* instead of the *balance*, this alternative framework allows us to examine the effects of global versus national business cycles. In addition, this framework points to the importance of the *components* of the trade flows (for example, consumer goods versus capital goods) in the long-run capacity of an economy to grow. Finally, this framework integrates the exchange rate and relative-price concepts elaborated in chapter 7.

Developing this framework is a first step toward addressing whether we are living beyond our means or are "an oasis of prosperity."[1] This chapter focuses mostly on the cyclical underpinnings of the trade deficit, although the persistent trend is addressed as well. Chapter 10 switches the focus to address whether the persistent trend and its trajectory are sustainable over the long term.

Income and Relative Prices Affect Trade Flows

Two key factors that drive trade flows are income growth and changes in relative prices. Exports grow faster when foreign income grows faster and when the relative prices of exports to competing goods and services in the destination market fall. Imports grow faster when domestic income grows faster and when the relative prices of imports to domestic goods and services fall (figure 8.2).

The relationship between GDP growth and trade is very obvious in the data. But close examination reveals the role of relative prices as well. Relative prices have several components: the cost of production, the firm's markup over cost, and the exchange rate, which allows a buyer to compare prices in a common currency (see chapter 7). The real exchange value of the US dollar summarizes these three factors. If costs and markups remain about unchanged, an appreciation of the dollar will reduce the price of imports into the United States and will make US exports more expensive in the destination market's currency. Thus when the dollar appreciated in the periods of 1975-77 and 1981-85, for example, the growth rate of US exports was less than or fell relatively more than would have been expected on the basis of the growth of foreign income (for these years, the dotted line above the solid line in figure 8.2b). In contrast, when the dollar depreciated, as in the 1977-79 and 1986-89 periods, the price of imports into the United States tended to rise, so import growth was less than would have been expected on the basis of the growth of US income (the dotted line above the solid line in figure 8.2a). The price of US exports in the destination market currency tended to fall, making US exports more attractive there, and so exports grew faster than would have been expected on the basis of world income (the dotted line below the solid line in figure 8.2b).

---

1. The phrase "oasis of prosperity" has been used by Alan Greenspan, the chairman of the Federal Reserve Board, in numerous speeches in 1998 and 1999 to describe the economic situation in the United States compared to its trading partners as well as to warn that the United States cannot remain such an oasis forever.

Figure 8.2 Economic growth, exchange rate, and trade balance, 1975-98

A. Imports and US GDP growth

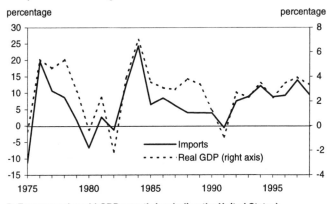

B. Exports and world GDP growth (excluding the United States)

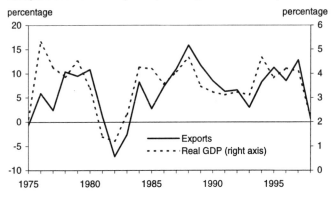

C. Real effective exchange rate, WPI-base

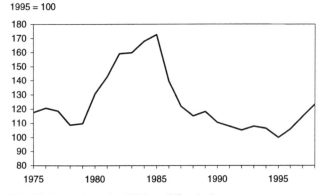

Note: World growth rate for 1998 is an IMF projection.
Sources: US Department of Commerce, *Survey of Current Business;* IMF, *International Financial Statistics; World Economic Outlook.*

This income and relative price framework for analyzing trade flows is incomplete in the sense that income and the components of relative prices and the exchange rate are not modeled along with exports and imports. Feedback mechanisms between trade and both income and the relative prices clearly are important.[2] Moreover, this framework does not explicitly incorporate more fundamental determinants of trade, such as tastes and factor endowments.[3] Finally, it does not incorporate the feedback effects of large trade deficits on the exchange rate, a topic reserved for chapters 9 and 10. Nevertheless, this framework has been quite effective in explaining most of the year-to-year movements in real exports and imports and therefore the balance of US trade.

Domestic interest rates and the dollar exchange rate are not modeled here along with trade flows, but they are key links between this framework and the savings-investment framework outlined in chapter 2. Foreign savings is not a residual balancing entry (as in the NIPA equation) but is affected by interest and exchange rates and expectations for them. Domestic investment is also a function of the domestic interest rate. So if foreigners want to invest in US assets because the rate of return to capital in the United States is high, the dollar will appreciate relative to what it would be otherwise, and the external deficit will be larger than it would be otherwise. By the same token, US interest rates will be lower than they would be otherwise, and US investment and income stronger. Thus there is consistency between the income-relative price framework analyzed in this chapter and the savings-investment framework analyzed in chapter 2.

Business Cycles and External Balance

Since trade flows depend on income growth here and abroad, US external balance is importantly influenced by the degree to which the domestic and foreign cycles of economic activity are synchronized. Figure 8.3 shows the US real trade balance and the year-to-year growth rates in foreign and US income. Two periods of cyclical behavior stand out. In the early 1980s and again in the early 1990s, US GDP growth slowed dramatically well before economic activity in the rest of the world slackened. As the United States entered recession, consumption and investment slowed and import growth fell, but exports to the world continued growing. As a result, the trade deficit narrowed. On the other hand, coming out of recessions, the United States burst into periods of sustained recovery while the rest of the world stagnated, and the trade deficit widened considerably.

---

2. Chapter 5 discusses how trade competition and exchange rates affect productivity growth and domestic inflation, which are key underpinnings of income and relative prices.

3. How these are reflected in trade patterns and US trade characteristics is covered in chapter 3.

Figure 8.3 Relative growth and the trade balance, 1975-98

A. US real trade balance
billions of US dollars

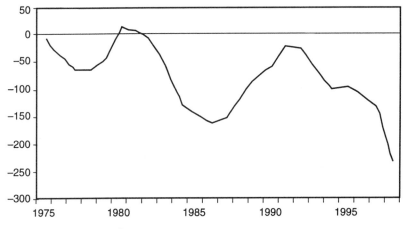

B. US and world growth rates
percentage

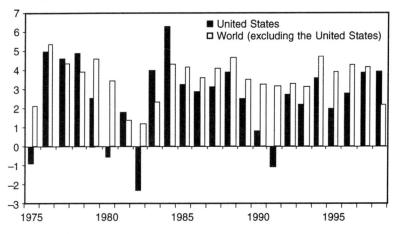

Sources: US Department of Commerce, *Survey of Current Business;* IMF, *International Financial Statistics* (1997).

This behavior is also evident in the late 1990s. The US economy slowed in 1994, but then rebounded and continued to strengthen from 1995 through 1998 (and into 1999). The world growth rate remained steady in the early 1990s, dipping just a bit in 1995 and then, of course, dropping dramatically into the trough generated by the financial crises of 1997-98. Consequently, US imports have tended to rise faster than US exports, causing the trade deficit to widen.

Just as the trade balance is influenced importantly by the difference between income growth at home and abroad, the trade balance also reflects the internal imbalance between domestic demand and production.[4] When domestic demand outstrips capacity to produce, as has been the case in the United States in the past several years, trade acts as a "safety valve," allowing domestic demand to be satisfied without generating inflationary pressures on prices (figure 8.4). The trade balance also acts to cushion production when domestic demand is weak. For example, in the mid-1990s, when domestic demand was not growing as strongly, GDP growth and employment were supported by increased exports abroad.

Impact of Financial Turmoil on US External Balances

The most recent and dramatic example of the effect of changes in domestic and global growth on the US trade and current account balances is the period of financial turmoil and associated US policy responses[5] (table 8.1). In early 1997, as the turmoil was brewing, the consensus forecast presented in the *OECD Economic Outlook*[6] (June 1997 issue) suggested that both the United States and the OECD member countries as a group would grow more rapidly than they had in 1996, with the increase in the US growth rate expected to be significantly greater than the OECD average. Consequently, the OECD analysis projected a widening of the US external deficit: the US merchandise trade deficit for 1997 was projected to be $205 billion, with the current account deficit at 2.3 percent of GDP.

At that time, the OECD projected that the expected robust growth in the United States would precipitate monetary tightening, which would slow the US economy substantially by 1998. Overall OECD growth was expected to retreat a bit too, but by far less than US growth, since the other member countries had not been growing as fast for so long. This constellation of US and OECD growth rates for 1998 was supposed to stabilize the US external deficit in 1998, with a merchandise trade deficit of $215 billion and the current account deficit at 2.4 percent of GDP.

What actually happened is quite different. By the time the December 1998 forecast was issued (with much of the data for the year already available), forecasters dramatically reduced their expectations for OECD growth

---

4. This presentation is another approach to examining the NIPA framework outlined in chapter 2.

5. Included in the rubric "financial turmoil" are the banking and currency crises in several emerging markets in Asia, the policy failures in Japan, and the Russian defaults on loans. The introduction of the euro adds uncertainty to this period.

6. The consensus forecast from the OECD member countries is representative of many forecasts; its use here should not highlight any particular folly or accuracy on the part of the OECD.

Figure 8.4 Trade as the "safety valve," 1991-99 (1Q)

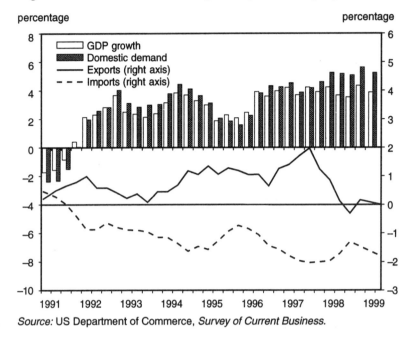

Source: US Department of Commerce, Survey of Current Business.

in 1998. But the US GDP growth rate, partly in response to significant *easing* of US monetary policy (in contrast to the tightening that had been expected), was one and one-half times what it had been projected to be 18 months earlier, and domestic demand growth stood at more than twice the projected rate. Imports were flowing into the United States. The projected drop in OECD growth, precipitated in part by the falloff in demand in the Asian markets, worsened, and half a percentage point was lopped off the OECD growth rate. US exports were expected to slump—and they did fall, starting at the end of 1998 and into the first three months of 1999. The US current account for 1998 was estimated to widen to −2.7 percent of GDP with a merchandise trade deficit of $256 billion, in contrast to the −2.4 percent and $215 billion that had been projected in early 1997, before the series of crises began. Finally, the actual data show even more dramatically the impact of the crises. The falloff in exports hit merchandise hardest, with the actual deficit recorded at $312 billion.

The forecasters have tended over the past 18 months to overestimate OECD growth and underestimate US growth. If this pattern continues, the external deficit will be significantly larger than currently projected. Indeed, forecasts based on data for the first quarter of 1999 project a merchandise trade deficit of $340 billion for the year. The consequences of a continued large deficit are addressed in more detail in chapter 10.

Table 8.1 Projected growth and US external balance, 1997-99

	1996	1997	1998	1999
	Actual	Projected	Projected	
Prediction in June 1997				
OECD growth (percentage, year-over-year)	3.0	3.0	2.7	–
US growth (percentage)	3.4	3.6	2.0	–
US domestic demand (percentage)	3.6	3.9	2.1	–
US current account				
Share of GDP (percentage)	-1.8	-2.3	-2.4	–
Level (billions of US dollars)	-134.9	-187	-202	–
US merchandise trade balance (billions of US dollars)	-198.0	-205	-215	–
			Estimated	**Projected**
Prediction in December 1998				
OECD growth (percentage)	–	–	2.2	1.7
US growth (percentage)	–	–	3.5	1.5
US domestic demand (percentage)	–	–	4.9	2
US current account				
Share of GDP (percentage)	–	–	-2.7	-3.1
Level (billions of US dollars)	–	–	-229	-272
US merchandise trade balance (billions of US dollars)	–	–	-256	-286
		Actual		
OECD growth (percentage, year-over-year)	3.0	3.2	2.2[a]	n.a.
US growth (percentage)	3.4	3.9	3.9	n.a.
US domestic demand (percentage)	3.6	4.2	5.2	n.a.
US current account				
Share of GDP (percentage)	-1.8	-1.9	-2.7	n.a.
Level (billions of US dollars)	-134.9	-155.2	-233.4	n.a.
US merchandise trade balance (billions of US dollars)	-198.0	-248.0	-311.9	n.a.

n.a. = not available
a. This figure is estimated.

Source: OECD Economic Outlook (June 1997, December 1998).

The Puzzling "Income Asymmetry"

There is a puzzling relationship between relative GDP growth rates and US trade flows. Although US economic activity rebounded and has been quite strong during periods of economic expansion in the 1980s and 1990s,

Table 8.2 Estimated income elasticities of trade for the United States

Investigators	Data period	Income elasticities	
		Exports of goods and services	Imports of goods and services
Houthakker and Magee (1969)	1951-66	0.99	1.51
Hooper, Johnson, and Marquez (1998)	1960-96	0.80 (long-run)	1.80 (long-run)
		1.80 (short-run)	1.00 (short-run)
Cline (1989)	1973-87	1.70	2.44

		Exports		Imports	
		Goods	Services	Goods	Services
Wren-Lewis and Driver (1998)	1980-95	1.21	1.95	2.36	1.72

its growth rate is still generally lower than the world growth rate (figure 8.3b). Yet the trade deficit has generally continued to widen. The puzzle—whereby the rest of the world grows faster than the United States but the United States still incurs a trade deficit—is a consequence of what apparently is a greater appetite for imports by US consumers and businesses than foreigners' appetite for US exports. This has been a feature of US trade for the whole of the postwar period, but the implications for the trade deficit have been more apparent since the breakdown of the Bretton Woods system of fixed exchange rates.

Econometric analyses of the joint effect of income and relative prices on the US trade balance have consistently estimated that US imports and exports respond to about the same degree to changes in relative prices, but differ significantly in their response to changes in economic activity. A variety of estimation periods, different data, and several techniques yield broadly the same results (table 8.2). The estimated responsiveness of US imports to US economic activity is significantly larger than the responsiveness of exports to changes in foreign economic activity, particularly in the long run and for trade in goods. This "income asymmetry" implies that even if the United States and its trading partners grow at the same rate (and the exchange value of the dollar remains unchanged), the US real trade deficit widens. In addition, while the estimate of the income elasticity varies a bit, generally it is larger than 1, which means that as income rises, imports rise more than proportionately.

These results are particularly interesting in that, although they have persisted since economists started examining the relationships in the early 1960s (with data going back to the first postwar years), they violate long-run principles. That is, in a theoretical "long-run global equilibrium," all countries will import at the same rate, since if a single country imported more than its share, it ultimately would consume the production of all other countries. There is a similar "long-run internal equilibrium" within a country by which income and imports should grow at the same rate, since if income did not keep pace, a country would ultimately spend all its income on imports.

In the context of the United States, a persistently higher import elasticity for the United States would imply that the world would absorb US assets while the United States consumed all its production. Moreover, with an income elasticity of imports greater than 1, as the United States grew, more and more of its income would be spent on imports, and more and more of its production would be exported, until there was no longer any domestic consumption of domestic production. Neither of these cases makes sense; nor do we see a trend in that direction for world trade and finance. Yet the econometric estimates of the income elasticities are very effective when it comes to projecting changes in US exports and imports.

Much research has focused on trying to explain the sources of the income asymmetry. For example, some researchers suggest that there is a "missing variable" in their econometric estimation procedure, or mismeasured variables. Candidate variables include new global capacity to produce, entry of new international competitors into the global marketplace, and incorrect price measures. Although promising in some instances, none of this work has resolved the income asymmetry (see Hooper and Mann 1989; Mann 1991).

A different approach is to consider whether the income asymmetry might gradually disappear as the world's economies mature and spend more on services and less on manufactured goods. Supporting this possibility is the observation that the income asymmetry is quite pronounced for US trade in goods, but is nearly absent (by one estimate even reversed) for US trade in services (see table 8.2). As foreign economies mature, some of their growing demand for services will spill over into purchases of US service exports. The share of service exports in total US exports of goods and services would increase, which would tend to increase the foreign income elasticity. Ensuring that these markets are open to receive US service exports will enhance the likelihood that this scenario will unfold. (For more on the service sector's role in US trade flows, trade policy, and the sustainability of the trade deficit, see chapters 3, 6, and 10.)

Finally, a combination of the "missing variable" and "long-term changes" research shows that demographic factors can both significantly affect the estimated income asymmetry and point to a reduction of the asymmetry in the future. Including demographic factors (such as immigrants and the age distribution of domestic residents) into the equation for US imports reduces the income elasticity of imports to the unity value expected (Marquez 1998, 1999; Gould 1994). These two demographic factors make sense, and they also help to explain why the trade deficit persists now. Immigrants certainly have more information about products available abroad and may maintain their tastes for native products long after moving to a new country. Foreign-born residents account for about 10 percent of the US population, twice the proportion of the 1960s. Ignoring a rising share of people who have a greater tendency to consume imports for any given income level would tend to bias upward the estimated relationship between income and imports. By the same token, older residents tend to consume a higher fraction of "domestic" goods and services such as health care. As this group grows as a proportion of the US population, income elasticity on imports of consumption goods would tend to fall.

Private Savings and the Components of Trade

In light of both historical behavior and recent developments, it is too simple to conclude that the existence of an external deficit means that the United States is living beyond its means. Changes in the external position are the product of both domestic and global forces. Nevertheless, after we have cut through the cyclical variations and considered possible structural change, two strands of evidence suggest longer-term problems, which might imply that a reduction in US spending will be necessary in the future to pay for our current period of consuming more than we produce.

The Behavior of Private Spending

The first strand of evidence is found in the correlation between the decline in the private savings rate and the behavior of the trade deficit (figure 8.5). Although not a close relationship on a year-to-year basis, the rate of private savings has generally trended downward since the early 1980s, which is about when the persistent trade gap opened up. Indeed, the reductions in the trade deficit in 1981-82 and 1991-92 resulted more from a cyclical slowdown in investment than from an increase in private savings (see figure 2.5). In recent years, the rate of personal savings by households has fallen even more dramatically, as has the trade balance, most notably the merchandise component. Thus the declining rate of private savings, driven particularly by declining household savings, might help to explain the persistence of the external deficit.[7]

But national income and product accounting shows that the trade balance mirrors the balance between *national* savings and investment, not *private* savings and investment (see chapter 2). Why would the decline in private savings, particularly personal savings, appear to cause the trade deficit to widen more than an increase in government savings would tend to make the trade balance narrow? The main reason is that the marginal

---

7. For discussions of possible mismeasurement of the household savings rate, see the references cited in chapter 2.

Figure 8.5 Private savings and trade balance, 1970-98

percentage of GDP

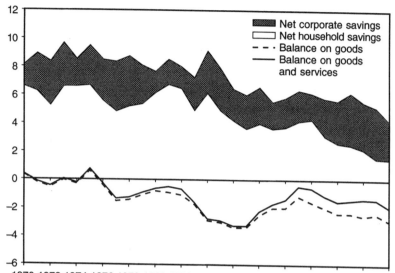

Source: US Department of Commerce, *Survey of Current Business.*

propensity of the government to consume imports is less than that of private businesses and households—that is, government saving and personal dis-saving have different first-round effects. Changes in the behavior of private market participants have a greater effect on the trade balance.

However, simply having a low savings rate does not necessarily imply difficulties in repaying what has been borrowed, as the examples of the corporation and the student at the beginning of this chapter suggest. What matters is what is being purchased by households and businesses when they buy instead of save. This requires examining the major components of trade as well as the overall pace of domestic consumption and investment.

The Components of Trade

Both the cyclical pattern and the persistent trend in the US trade balance are related to two key categories of trade in goods. First, recall that the behavior of the overall balance comes from the cycle and trend in the balance on merchandise trade (see figure 3.2). The cyclical behavior of the balance on merchandise trade comes from fluctuations in trade in capital goods and industrial supplies and materials, which are the two components most associated with the changes in businesses' demand for investment goods that occur over the business cycle. On the other hand, the per-

Figure 8.6 Balance on merchandise trade by sector, 1975-98

billions of US dollars

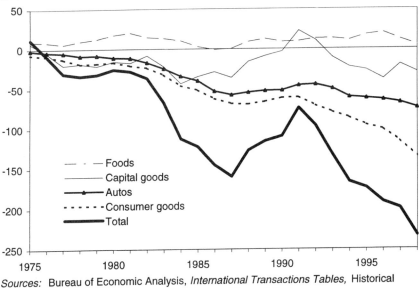

Sources: Bureau of Economic Analysis, *International Transactions Tables*, Historical Diskette; US Department of Commerce, *Survey of Current Business*.

sistent downward trend in the trade balance comes from a widening deficit in consumer goods and autos (figure 8.6). This suggests that consumers have been driving the trend not just by spending generally, but in particular by spending on imported consumption goods and autos. This pattern of spending on imported consumption goods matches domestic consumer spending habits, as evidenced by retail sales data. Such spending, however, does not appear to be of the sort that will finance the wherewithal to repay the associated borrowing.

Examining imports alone yields a somewhat different assessment (table 8.3). In the early 1980s, the fastest-growing component of imports was consumer goods and autos, at somewhat less than twice the rate of growth of merchandise imports over the period. In contrast, in the 1990s, import growth has been balanced between consumer goods and autos on the one hand and investment goods of capital machinery and industrial supplies and materials on the other. Returning to the analogy of the firm investing in plant and equipment, in the 1990s US imports seem to be of the type that will support the capacity of the United States to grow, which should create the wherewithal to make good on the financial investments purchased by foreigners as well as by domestic investors. This pattern of investment imports matches the robust investment demand in the United States in the 1990s.

Table 8.3 Growth rate of US merchandise imports
(percentage, period average)

	1982-87	1991-98
Total	7.9	8.0
Consumer goods and autos	16.8	8.1
Capital goods and industrial supply materials	10.4	10.0
Foods	5.2	6.0
Energy products	-7.8	0.3
Other	14.3	9.3

Source: US Department of Commerce, *International Transactions Tables.*

What are we to conclude from the data? Cyclical spending is robust, the rest of the world is growing slowly, and this is why the trade deficit has continued to widen. In comparison to the 1980s, the pattern of spending in the 1990s is better balanced between consumption and investment goods, so the cyclical widening of the deficit in the 1990s is of less concern than it was in the 1980s. Hence, for the time being, the United States is an oasis of prosperity. However, the underlying persistent trend decline in the external balance and its association with a persistent decline in personal savings are trends that cannot continue and that will sow the seeds of change in either incomes or relative prices (exchange rates)—points that will be addressed in the final chapter. Hence, from the long-term perspective, the United States is living beyond its means.

Conclusion

Summary

- At any point in time, the trade balance is a reflection of short-run cyclical behavior of income growth here and abroad as well as of trends in saving and spending. Thus a trade deficit by itself does not indicate that the United States is spending beyond its means.

- From the global perspective, the dramatic widening of the deficit in the late 1990s is fundamentally of a cyclical nature, being driven by a continued robust US economy while the rest of the world stagnates or drops into recession. Moreover, the impact of the differential in rates of growth of GDP on the trade balance has been augmented by an appreciation of the dollar of some 25 percent since mid-1995.

- From the domestic perspective, the trade balance acts as a "safety valve." Imports satisfy robust domestic demand when it exceeds domestic production, as it certainly has recently, and exports support domestic production when domestic demand is weak.

■ The trend decline in the private savings rate, particularly of the personal household savings rate, appears to be importantly associated with the trend widening of the trade deficit. The improvement in the government savings rate in the late 1990s (from the shift into surplus of the federal budget balances) has not offset the decline in the private savings rate, because smaller proportions of government spending go to imported goods and services.

■ In principle, a lower private savings rate could mean that certain kinds of spending are being undertaken that will raise the future growth rate of the economy, enabling it to service the debt incurred by the spending program. In the past decade, investment goods have increased as a share of trade, and the growth rate of investment and imports of investment goods all have been quite robust. Consequently, the trend widening of the deficit during the 1990s may be more easily financed by new capacity in the US economy in comparison to the widening trade deficit of the 1980s, which was associated with falling rates of investment.

Policy Discussion

■ Statistical analysis has long documented an asymmetry in the relationship between US growth and imports versus foreign growth and exports that implies a persistently widening trade deficit. This asymmetry is particularly pronounced for merchandise trade, but it is less apparent (or reversed) for trade in services. Consequently, as foreign economies develop and begin to consume a higher fraction of services, US total exports should begin to grow even more quickly. Trade negotiations to liberalize the service sector would help to ensure that US companies have a fair shot at these developing markets.

■ The United States is an oasis of prosperity that, to some extent, it has created by spending beyond its means. Much of the spending has been on investment in computers and information technology, which is increasing the long-run capacity of the economy to grow and hence is not profligate. Nevertheless, the trend decline in personal savings and the dependence on wealth for consumption and consumer-goods imports creates a vulnerability. This consumption path cannot be maintained unless wealth growth and foreign savings continue on their present courses, which neither is likely to do in perpetuity.

9

Do International Capital Markets Determine a Country's Trade Balance?

The market is fueled and foiled by deregulated capital transactions, with over a trillion dollars a day changing hands in foreign exchange markets, many times that needed to finance trade or real investment.

—John J. Sweeney, President of the AFL-CIO, remarks at
the Council on Foreign Relations (1 April 1998)

The new international financial system . . . has been, despite recent setbacks, a major factor in the marked increase in living standards for those economies that have chosen to participate in it. It has done so by facilitating cross-border trade in goods and services that has enhanced competition and expanded the benefits of the international division of labor.

—Alan Greenspan, chairman of the Federal Reserve Board, remarks at
the annual meeting of the Securities Industry Association,
Boca Raton, Florida (5 November 1998)

During the 1990s there has been one international financial-market crisis after another: the breakdown of the European Exchange Rate Mechanism (ERM) in 1992-93, the Mexican peso crisis of 1994-95, the Asian financial turbulence that started in 1997, the Russian financial collapse in 1998. In each case, the outflow of international capital required a complementary move of the trade account toward or into surplus. Do these episodes imply that international capital flows are the real driver of the external accounts? Are the models of external balance based on national savings and investment (chapter 2) or of trade flows based on income and relative prices (chapter 8) obsolete for determining a country's current account? Is it the desire for portfolio diversification and then the fickleness of expectations for risk and return that really matter?

Technological change in the finance industry has combined with the post-Bretton Woods flexible exchange rate regime to affect the relationship between international capital flows and international trade flows. The dramatic increase in the range of financial instruments made available by financial technology contributes to the huge gross flows of financial capital that can move very rapidly into and out of currencies and investments. However, the capital account and the current account must balance: changes in net capital flows must be reflected in changes in the trade account (plus net investment payments on the net international investment position). So the real question is, How do the forces of global capital affect the economic channels that equilibrate the current and capital accounts?

While the current and capital accounts respond to the same underlying economic forces associated with income growth and relative price changes, they do so in different time frames. These forces are reflected in asset prices such as interest rates and exchange rates nearly immediately, but they work to change real flows of trade in goods and services much more slowly because of the different speed of adjustment of financial flows compared to real flows. In addition, *expectations* for a country's profile of risk and return (which is another way of describing income and relative prices) are particularly important in the quick-response market of financial capital. When real or expected performance changes, a tension develops between the very rapid response of financial flows and the slower response of trade flows. This tension invariably will be reflected in the prices that can adjust most quickly and freely, that is, asset prices, particularly market-driven exchange rates.

There is no surefire recipe for keeping expectations and activity stable and avoiding the consequences of the mismatch between the rapid responsiveness of financial capital and the slower responsiveness of real resources. However, an appropriate mix of fiscal and monetary policy keeps the macroeconomy on the right track. A transparent and sound financial system with sufficient prudential reserves and an adequate range of financial instruments helps to avoid surprises, prevent destabilizing financial flows, and improve the allocation and diversification of domestic and international capital to the benefit of real growth.

Trade, Finance, and External Crises: Common Features from the Gold Standard, to Bretton Woods, to the 1990s

Under the theory of the gold standard of international exchange, international trade and capital flows were tightly related through the *price-specie flow mechanism.* If the value of exports from a particular country exceeded the value of imports from that country, gold (the medium of financial transactions) would flow from the net importer to the net exporter. More gold would increase the money supply (under the rules of the gold standard), prices and income would rise in the net exporting country, and imports would increase until trade was rebalanced. The reverse flows and forces would be at work in the net importing country. Trade imbalances in both countries would adjust, and flows of gold reserves would be the financial transaction in the capital account. In this simple world, trade imbalances generated financial flows that changed economic activity so as to rebalance the external sector.

The principles of international trade and finance under the gold standard from about 1880 to 1913 were not dissimilar from the theory, but the operation was quite different. In fact, very little gold flowed from one country to another.[1]

The theory of how the Bretton Woods gold-exchange system would operate was similar, except that international reserves of a convertible currency took the place of gold. The currencies' value in terms of gold was also fixed (although it could be adjusted), and hence the Bretton Woods system has also been called the fixed-but-adjustable exchange rate system.[2]

Trade imbalances driven by income and relative prices tended to dominate financial flows. In theory, a trade deficit would lead to the outflow of international reserves, which reduced the money supply, income, and wealth. Imports would fall, and the trade gap would close.[3] For the net exporter, the inflows of international reserves might lead to an economic expansion and more imports, but not necessarily. The net exporter could choose to stockpile the inflow of foreign assets and insulate the domestic economy from the increased money supply. Unlike the net importer, the net exporter did not face a constraint on its ability to hold reserves— although it might decide that it no longer wanted to hold the additional assets issued by the net importing country. Indeed, the proximate cause of the breakdown of the Bretton Woods system of fixed exchange rates based on dollar parities was the combination of US unwillingness to adjust domestic policies and other countries' unwillingness to increase their holdings of US financial assets.

In the early postwar period the United States assisted in the reconstruction of Europe with the Marshall Plan and of Japan with the Dodge

---

1. For more on the period of the gold standard, see Cooper (1982).

2. For a discussion of the origin and operation of the Bretton Woods system, see Levich (1998, 22-31).

3. For a time, the central bank in the net importer could insulate the money supply and the economy from the fall in reserves by augmenting domestic credit and short-circuiting the adjustment mechanisms. But ultimately international reserves would be used up, and the country would have to undergo the contraction necessary to bring the trade account back into balance.

Plan. A relatively more open US market encouraged trade flows. On the monetary side, as part of the underpinnings of Bretton Woods, the United States committed both to maintain a stable price level and to exchange dollars into gold at $35 per ounce.[4] Robert Triffin (1960) noted the inevitable clash between these objectives early on (figure 9.1).

While the US policies generally were good for the world and for the United States, they were not sustainable. On the one hand, US policy was achieving international price stability, and global growth was higher on average. But on the other hand, the domestic imbalance from fiscal spending, first on the Korean conflict and then on the Vietnam War and the Great Society programs, ultimately was reflected in an external trade imbalance. Foreign holdings of US assets clearly were on a trajectory to exceed the value of US gold reserves, which undermined the commitment to exchange those liabilities into gold at the fixed-dollar price. As long as the external obligations were willingly held, the United States did not have to change its policy. But the one-way bet against the dollar-gold parity escalated after 1968 as foreign holdings of US assets exploded. Ultimately the conflict between US domestic policy and foreign countries' financial portfolio preferences caused the Bretton Woods system to collapse in 1973.

Changes in the 1990s:
Flexible Exchange Rates and
Computer Technology Enhance Capital Flows

The lessons of the Triffin Dilemma are as salient now as they were in the 1960s: Internal imbalances are reflected in trade deficits and an increase in net assets held by foreigners. At some point, investors may not want to buy additional assets. A reduced ability to borrow from abroad leads to the changes in income and relative prices (and investment and savings) necessary to rectify the trade imbalance and bring supply and demand for financial assets back into equilibrium.

What is different in today's environment? Most fundamentally, exchange rates are no longer fixed. Consequently, the channels of transmission of economic forces to income, relative prices, and the trade balance are somewhat different from those of the fixed-exchange-rate regimes. Second, trade and financial transactions are more independent of each other than in the Bretton Woods or the gold standard periods. One consequence of this independence is that the magnitude of financial flows dwarfs that of trade flows. Moreover, financial flows can move very rap-

---

4. The commitment to $35 per ounce was a way of pinning down the value of the dollar, against which all the other dollar parities would then be priced. A fixed-dollar price of gold became the nominal anchor to the international price level.

Figure 9.1 The Triffin Dilemma and the breakdown of Bretton Woods

A. Global growth and inflation

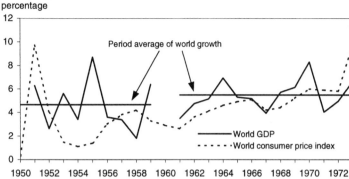

percentage

Note: Growth rate for 1960 is out of range because of the data inconsistency.
Sources: National Bureau of Economic Research (after Summers and Heston 1991)
<http://www.nber.org/pwt56.html> (30 December 1998); IMF, *International Financial Statistics Yearbook* (1979).

B. US fiscal and trade imbalances

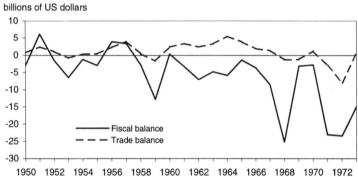

billions of US dollars

Sources: US Department of Commerce, *International Transactions Tables;* Council of Economic Advisers, *Economic Report of the President.*

C. US gold reserves and US liabilities to foreigners

billions of US dollars

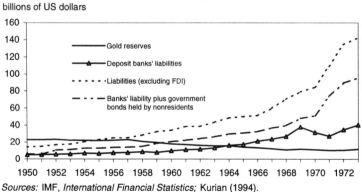

Sources: IMF, *International Financial Statistics;* Kurian (1994).

idly now, which puts a premium on stable policy and stable expectations. Offering one-way bets in the foreign exchange markets for an extended period (as was the case in Triffin's time) is no longer feasible.[5]

Flexible exchange rates alter the transmission from external shock or imbalances to the domestic economy by adding another equilibrating mechanism. In the simple world of an economic model, a trade deficit leads to a global excess supply of that country's currency. With everything else equal, the exchange rate (representing the relative prices of two currencies) should undergo pressure to depreciate because of this excess supply; with freely floating rates, it can do so. Then the exchange rate change passes through to affect the relative prices of imports and exports (as shown in the stylized example in table 7.1 and with data in chapter 8). Purchasers respond to these relative price changes; imports fall, exports rise, and the trade balance returns to equilibrium. This channel differs from that of the fixed-exchange-rate system in that a change in the exchange rate is the fulcrum for changing relative prices; in the earlier systems, the flows of gold or reserves changed the money supply, which then generated a change in domestic prices and thus in relative prices of traded goods. A simple distinction between the world of flexible exchange rates and that of fixed exchange rates is that with flexible rates relative prices can change more quickly.

Computer technology has further enhanced the role for exchange rates and capital-market flows. Flexible exchange rates create incentives for financial transactions that are completely divorced from trade transactions. Computer technology combined with analytical models (such as the options price formula) gives financial intermediaries the ability to create new financial instruments to meet the new demand. Some of these instruments remove the unwanted exchange risk (swaps) or insure against it (options and future-dated contracts). Others meet the business demand to take on more exchange risk than would be created by any underlying real transactions.

In addition, as financial wealth has increased in many countries, so has the desire for international portfolio diversification. Consequently, there is a greater demand for international financial instruments as well as a greater ability and willingness to supply them.[6] When played out in the many different markets for financial assets (such as currencies, bonds, equities, and derivatives), the gross value of financial transactions is enormous and increasing every year (table 9.1). From the standpoint of exchange rate movement, the increase in transactions based on financial demand adds to the real-trade-based demand for currency. To the extent

---

5. A good review of the literature on "speculative attacks" can be found in Garber and Svensson (1995).

6. See Frankel and Mann (1986) for a discussion of how financial institutions can remake themselves to meet new market demands.

Table 9.1 Dimensions of international capital markets in the 1990s
(billions of US dollars)

	1989	1992	1995	1996	1997
Foreign exchange market (daily turnover)[a]	718	1,076	1,572	n.a.	1,971[b]
International bond net new issuance	171.6	116.1	311.5	543.4	595.8
Equity market turnover ratio (percentage)[c]	63.8	43.8	57.5	66.7	82.8
Currency swaps outstanding	449.1	860.4	1,197.4	1,559.6	n.a.

n.a. = not available

a. Total reported turnover net of local double-counting (from Bank for International Settlements, *Central Bank Survey of Foreign Exchange and Derivatives Market Activity in April 1998*, table 2).

b. 1998 data.

c. Annual trading value/market capitalization (International Finance Corporation, *Emerging Stock Markets Factbook*, 1998).

Sources: Bank for International Settlements; International Finance Corporation.

that investors change their portfolios of assets more frequently than traders in real goods change their use of a particular currency, exchange rates and therefore relative prices will become more volatile.

Sophisticated financial intermediation implies that investors can target quite specifically the types of risk they wish to undertake. The returns on assets of different countries, in different currencies, and at different maturities are imperfectly correlated with each other and with the returns on financial assets of the home country and currency. The investor who holds a diversified portfolio can achieve a higher return for lower risk than would be possible with domestic financial assets alone. Consequently the "gains from trade" are no longer measured simply in the "real" domain of product price and variety; the gains from trade can also be measured along the "financial" domain of the risk-return frontier of the international capital assets pricing model.[7]

Indeed, in recent years, the deregulation of foreign financial markets and the desire to diversify portfolios have supported both greater demand by US residents for foreign stocks and bonds and foreign demand for US stocks and bonds. The regional decomposition of US net purchases of long-term securities reveals continued diversification of the securities portfolio in line with risk and return. The share of the US portfolio accounted for by investments in Europe is still large, but has shrunk as investors increasingly have purchased long-term investments in Asia (excluding Japan) and Latin America, where the gains from diversification are greater (figure 9.2).

Despite the rapid growth of international investments by US holders of wealth, the share of foreign assets in US wealth remains relatively small,

---

7. See the discussion of the gains from trade in financial assets in chapter 3. For a more comprehensive discussion, see Levich (1998, chaps. 11-16).

Figure 9.2 Net purchase of long-term foreign securities by US residents, by region, 1985-98

billions of US dollars

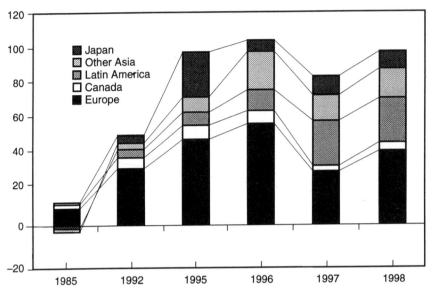

Note: Data do not necessarily reflect the domicile of the ultimate issuers of securities.

Source: US Treasury Department, *Treasury Bulletin;* <http://www.treas.gov/tic/ticsec.shtml> (14 July 1998).

about 7 percent (figure 9.3). Moreover, even when diversification is measured as the flow of net purchases of foreign assets as a share of the increase in total financial wealth of US residents, the exposure of US wealth to foreign financial instruments is small, though increasing. This "home bias," the preference for residents to hold wealth in assets issued by their own governments, firms, and banks, is well known and not unique to the United States (Lewis 1995).

The two sides of the balance of payments remain linked, however. In the end, any external trade deficit is financed by *net* capital inflows. Data measuring the current account and net flows of capital should be equal; the current account builds up the need for external financing from the trade side, and the capital account builds up the net capital flows from transactions in different types of financial assets. The two measures generally track each other, although net private capital flows are more volatile from quarter to quarter. The difference between these two measures of net financial resource flows from abroad, referred to as the external statistical discrepancy, has been quite large in some recent periods (figure 9.4). Indeed, in

Figure 9.3 Purchases and holdings of foreign financial assets as share of US total financial assets, 1980-98

percentage

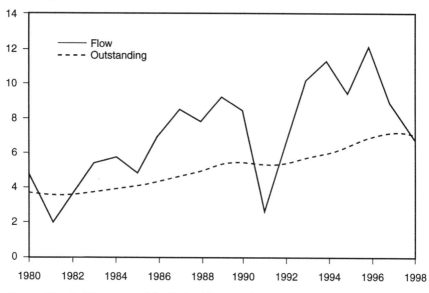

Source: Board of Governors of the Federal Reserve System, *Flow of Funds Accounts of the United States.*

recent years, the capital account measure as a share of GDP shows a more pronounced downward trend than the current account measure shows.[8]

An Illustration: Transmitting the Asian Financial Crises to US Capital Markets

Examining the impact of the Asian financial crises on the United States offers a good illustration of how capital flows are transmitted to exchange

8. A negative statistical discrepancy (meaning that net capital inflows exceed the current account deficit), such as has been the case for the past several years, represents some combination of unrecorded net capital outflows and net current account payments. On the trade side, illegal imports or unrecorded exports of goods or services would contribute to a negative statistical discrepancy. On the financial side, unrecorded US purchases of foreign financial instruments or overstated foreign purchases of US financial investments would also yield a negative statistical discrepancy. While individual episodes can be tied, on an ad hoc basis, to certain events (such as the large discrepancy in 1997, attributable to the financial turmoil in Asia), in general the behavior of the external statistical discrepancy is not well understood.

Figure 9.4 External statistical discrepancy: Difference between current account and net capital flows, 1960-98

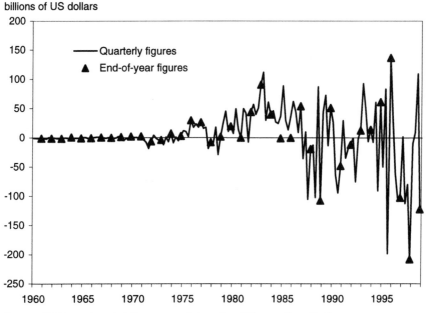

billions of US dollars

rates and interest rates to affect the trade account (figure 9.5). The series of crises started in Thailand in mid-1997 and culminated in Russia's default on its external debt in August 1998. Foreign private investors' "flight to quality assets" led them to purchase US government securities (which increased the inflow of capital to the United States) and also shifted the US domestic investor's portfolio toward US government securities. Interest rates fell on US government securities (figure 9.5a). The dollar continued to appreciate as investors bought dollars to purchase US assets (figure 9.5b). The appreciation of the dollar lowered import prices further and raised export prices in the currencies of the destination markets (figure 9.5c). Moreover, lower interest rates bolstered US economic activity, which boosted imports, while slack demand abroad hampered exports. Both the changes in relative prices and the differences in relative income induced by the crises widened the trade deficit. Hence the increased demand for US assets by foreigners worked through both interest rates and exchange rates to yield a wider trade deficit and a matching higher capital account.

Until investor sentiment toward US financial assets changes, these dynamics of foreign capital investment, an appreciated dollar, and a large trade deficit likely will continue. At some point, though, foreign investors will seek higher returns elsewhere, the capital inflows will slow, the dollar will depreciate, and the trade and current account deficits will narrow.

Figure 9.5 US capital account dynamics during Asian crises

A. International capital flows and bond yields

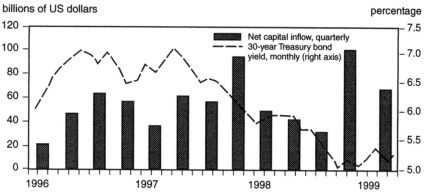

Sources: US Treasury Department, *Treasury Bulletin;* Federal Reserve Board.

B. Value of the dollar

1995 = 100

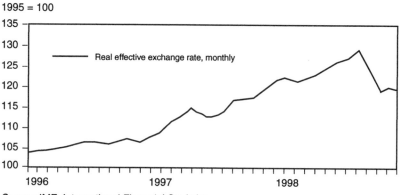

Source: IMF, *International Financial Statistics.*

C. Import and export prices and trade balance

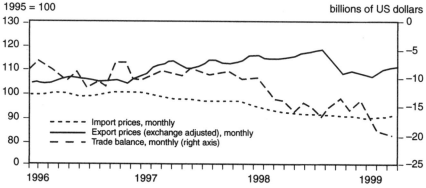

Note: Export price is adjusted to the currency of the importer by multiplying by the trade-weighted exchange rate.

Sources: US Bureau of Labor Statistics, *Export and Import Price Index;* US Department of Commerce, *International Trade Goods and Services.*

The question of when investors might make such a decision is addressed in chapter 10. Whether the process will be precipitous or smooth depends in large part on how rapidly financial markets adjust to changes that are taking place in consumption and investment here and abroad.

Differences in Response and Adjustment: The J-Curve and Financial Market Overshooting

Investors, producers, and consumers all respond to economic stimuli, such as asset price, production cost, product price, demand situation, and expectations for all of these. In principle, each of these actors can perceive changes in these variables equally quickly, since they all have access to the same information through newspapers, radio, television, and the Internet. However, not all of them can or would want to act on that information, in part because the relevance of a particular piece of information for an economic decision differs from one person or business to another.

One difference in reaction time is clear: financial flows respond more quickly to economic news and forces than do production and consumption. The mismatch in the underlying speed of adjustment of financial capital versus of real trade during periods of rapid movements in financial capital can precipitate excessive movements in the asset prices (exchange rate and interest rate), as these must overshoot their long-run change so as to generate enough movement in income and wealth, which determine trade flows.[9]

How quickly can capital move? In just a few years, computer technology has allowed real-time pricing of complex financial instruments—effectively creating markets for financial instruments that previously did not exist. In 1992 a foreign exchange trader completed a transaction about every 67 seconds (Lyons 1995). Electronic trading captured 5 percent of trading on foreign exchanges just two years after it was introduced in 1995 (Levich 1998, 89; Bank for International Settlements 1998, 19-20). Internet trading has exploded, recently reaching a volume of one in every six shares traded (*Economist*, 8 May 1999).

On the other hand, adjustment of demand and production to an exchange rate change occurs slowly, with a time lag. This characteristic pattern of the balance-of-payments adjustment to an exchange rate depreciation has been given the descriptive name "J-curve"—indicating that the

---

9. Changes in interest rates and exchange rates—in particular, expectations for these variables—affect rates of return on financial assets immediately, so adjustment in financial flows is rapid. Changes in interest rates and exchange rates affect trade and the flows of real resources more slowly, because real flows respond to income and wealth (not directly to the interest rate) and to relative prices (not just to the exchange rate).

trade balance worsens before it improves—and the process plays out over quarters and years, not minutes.[10]

The mismatch in these paces of response and adjustment is most apparent when investor sentiment changes swiftly and financial flows move much more rapidly than real flows can respond. For example, investor sentiment toward investing in South Korea changed radically near the end of 1997 as information on the state of local banking systems and international reserve holdings became apparent. Capital flows reversed dramatically from an inflow of some $5 billion per quarter in the first half of 1997 to an outflow of $20 billion in November. The collapse of foreign credit as well as domestic credit constrained economic activity. The exchange rate responded to this dramatic reduction in demand for won and increase in demand for US dollars, and the won's exchange value was cut in half (figure 9.6). The exchange rate moved so dramatically in order to force adjustment in growth and trade. When trade began to respond (not just to the relative prices, but also to the collapse of domestic demand as well as other institutional factors), the depreciation of the won was arrested and subsequently was partially reversed.

The Financial Turmoil of the 1990s: A Preview for the United States?

The recent volatility of international capital flows has rekindled the question of whether or not economic activity is best served by the current environment of relatively unfettered global financial markets. In today's global environment, national economic well-being increasingly relies on global production, distribution, consumption, and the web of international financial transactions that binds them all together. The real question, then, is how to make the financial markets work better. The recipe has certain definite ingredients. First, participants who have full information are more likely to assess and price risk appropriately, and thus they will be better prepared to respond to shocks. Second, if market participants are heterogeneous in their desires for risk and return and can employ a full set of financial instruments that spans the spectrum of risks, then there is less likely to be "herding" among investors.

---

10. Suppose the dollar depreciates. In the first quarter, about 40 percent of the change in the dollar's value will be reflected in the import and export prices. It will take about two years, however, for the change in relative prices induced by the exchange rate movement to complete its effect on demand for imports and exports. Consequently, soon after the depreciation, import prices are higher but demand has not yet responded, so the value of imports rises. At the same time, whereas prices in their own currency are lower, foreigners have not yet responded by buying more, so the value of exports does not rise immediately. The value of imports increases, but the value of exports does not, and the trade deficit initially widens until the change in relative prices induces the change in demand. When the real adjustment takes place, the trade account turns and moves toward surplus, thus completing the J shape.

Figure 9.6 Exchange rate overshooting: The case of South Korea

Note: Financial account is a part of capital account and represents financial transactions only.
Source: Bank of Korea <http://www.bok.or.kr/kb/index_e.html> (February 1999).

What was missing to cause the recent turmoil? Differentiation among recipients of international capital flows was made more difficult by incomplete or incorrect information, revealed only very slowly by certain borrowers. In addition, banks in the recipient countries did not adequately provision against the potentially volatile nature of the foreign currency deposit base.[11]

At the same time, investors behaved like a herd. The very narrow risk spreads on emerging market debt in early 1997 and the huge risk spreads on even the best corporate borrowers after the Russian default point to a lack of differentiation as well a swing in collective sentiment completely out of line with changes in the underlying economic prospects of many of the countries (and companies) caught in the financial maelstrom (figure 9.7).

Moreover, the market for financial instruments is also incomplete. It lacks financial insurance against the rare events of credit downgrade or restructuring (e.g., delay in payment or rollover) of short-term obligations in particular. Similarly, bond contracts do not address how the obligation

---

11. For a comprehensive discussion of the Asian financial crises and the role of the domestic banking systems, see Goldstein (1998).

Figure 9.7 Herding in financial markets: Risk spreads in three bond markets

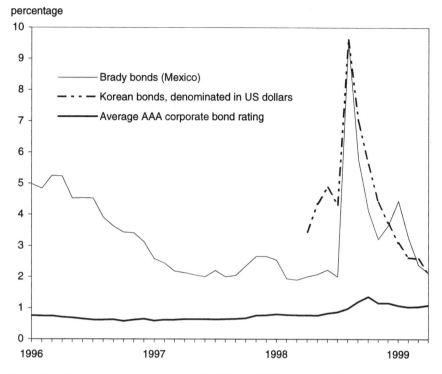

percentage

Note: The risk spread is calculated using the 30-year US Treasury bond rate.

Sources: Federal Reserve System <http://www.bog.frb.fed.us/releases/G13/>; Bloomberg <http://www.bloomberg.com>.

should be treated in the case of restructuring.[12] Financial insurance instruments, such as credit risk insurance or restructuring insurance, or augmented bond contracts could help to stabilize the international financial system (Mann 1999).

Does the large US trade deficit make the United States vulnerable to herding, capital flight, and a dollar crash? The US economy is not immune from herding—indeed, the impact of the crises on US Treasury bond rates and dollar appreciation shows how financial herding during the Asian crises affected US asset prices. And US monetary authorities did take aggressive action to reduce interest rates in the fall of 1998 after the Russian default. On the whole, however, the United States is different in its ability to absorb herding behavior, and is special in that it both borrows

---

12. For more discussion of changes to bond contracts, see Eichengreen (1999, esp. chap. 5).

and lends principally in its own currency. While a depreciation of the dollar could happen—and, indeed, is likely—a crash is unlikely, because the dollar and US investments are so important to global finance and in global portfolios. The implications of these and other issues for sustainability are addressed in the next chapter.

Conclusion

Summary

- The underlying economic forces that drive trade flows and capital flows are the same as they were under the gold standard and the Bretton Woods system: income, relative prices, savings, and investment.

- However, the environment of flexible exchange rates and sophisticated financial intermediaries has made capital transactions largely independent of trade transactions. Gross volumes of capital transactions far exceed trade transactions. *Annual* volume of global trade about doubled during the 1990s; *daily* financial transactions increased threefold.

- With the globalization of financial wealth, the "gains from trade" should no longer be seen only in the familiar terms of product price and variety of goods and services. The gains from globalization also include the superior risk-return profile of the allocation of financial wealth allowed by international diversification.

Policy Discussion

- Because capital flows are much larger and more rapidly mobile than before, stable policies, and particularly stable expectations, are critical. Mismatched macroeconomic policies generate internal and external imbalances that are more difficult to sustain, and the longer the imbalances persist in the real markets, the more dramatic the reaction in financial markets when it comes.

- The United States is not immune from changes in investor sentiment, but it is better able to weather panics. First, currency mismatch is less of a problem for the United States, since much borrowing is dollar based. Second, asset markets are deep, quite liquid, and populated by diverse investors. Finally, because US dollar assets are so important in the global web of finance and in global investors' portfolios, changes in investor sentiment that have an impact on interest rates or the exchange value of the dollar are more likely to be self-righting than would be the case for countries whose assets represent the fringe of an investor's portfolio instead of the heart of it.

10

Is the US External Deficit Sustainable?

Over the longer run ... the persistence of large trade deficits could cause foreign investors to shift out of dollar assets—perhaps precipitously.

—Gene Koretz, *Business Week* (23 February 1998)

[T]his deficit has a very different character from the imbalances of the mid-1980s. . . . [T]he U.S. trade gap is "self-financing" to a greater extent than were the deficits of the 1980s.

—Chase Currency Research, *Special Report* (6 April 1998)

[T]he international system cannot sustain indefinitely the large current account imbalances created by the disparities in growth and openness between the U.S. and its major trading partners.

—Treasury Secretary Robert Rubin, press conference before G-7 meeting (17 February 1999)

Whenever a country's current account deficit grows large, questions arise as to how large it can get, how long it can persist, and what forces might either stabilize it or cause it to shrink. The history of financial crises from Latin America in the 1890s to Asia in the 1990s, and plenty of industrialized countries in between, clearly shows that too much external borrowing and/or accumulated international obligations can precipitate financial and, subsequently, economic disasters. But what is it that precipitates the crisis? Is it the size of the deficit or accumulated obligations? Do their particular characteristics (such as maturity or currency) or their use (such as for consumption or real estate ventures) contribute to the economic forces that precipitate a crisis? Moreover, when the current account deficit gets large, is crisis inevitable, or are more benign outcomes possible?

Answering the question of whether the US current account deficit and net international investment position are sustainable requires some preliminary analytical and empirical groundwork. We must define "sustainable," and we must do so from two related perspectives: that of the net borrower—the United States—and that of the net investor—the rest of the world. (A third dimension, political sustainability, will be discussed as well.) On the borrower's side, analyses of different countries' experiences with large current account deficits and net international obligations can help to uncover empirical evidence of what constitutes sustainability. But will these be applicable to the United States, or do different rules apply to the United States because of the international role of the dollar or the size and strength of the US economy?

On the investor side, we must look at the size and composition of global wealth portfolios. How important are US dollar obligations in the portfolios of potential investors? Can the US dollar share in world portfolio holdings grow larger than might be the case for some other countries' assets because the United States is so important in global trade and finance? What we find is that it is not only how much the United States can and does borrow that matters for the deficits' sustainability but also how much investors in other countries are willing to buy and hold US assets in their portfolios of financial assets. The United States is special in both regards.

This chapter begins with a framework for assessing sustainability and then applies it to data from the United States and from other industrial countries. I then construct trajectories for the trade account, the current account, and the net international investment position under three different scenarios. The first scenario assumes that the exchange value of the dollar remains at the high levels of 1998 and early 1999 and that US and world growth rates return to long-term rates of growth of potential. I compare the values for the external accounts to sustainability benchmarks taken from US experience as well as from the experience of other industrialized countries. Whether the United States is special—and if so, in what way—is an important part of assessing whether the constellation of growth and exchange value of the dollar assumed in this scenario yields sustainable trajectories of external balance and position.

In the second scenario, I review what would happen to the trajectory of external accounts and their relationship to sustainability benchmarks if the dollar were to depreciate substantially. The amount of depreciation is chosen by how much it would take to return the dollar to an estimate of the fundamental equilibrium exchange rate (Wren-Lewis and Driver 1998).

The third scenario focuses on structural change in the international environment. Specifically, the third trajectory shows the implications for US external accounts if the exchange value of the dollar remained unchanged, if economic reforms increased US and world rates of growth of potential, and if liberalization and deregulation of service sectors worldwide increased US services exports as a share of total exports.

The Concept of Sustainability

"Sustainable" in the context of the economics of external balance refers to "stasis," that is, a stable state or a stable path where the external balance generates no economic forces of its own to change its trajectory. A sustainable external balance is one in which the feedback relationships between the external balance and exchange rates and interest rates are relatively weak in comparison to other macroeconomic forces that affect these asset prices. For example, a large current account deficit may make investors worry that they might not be repaid. They might then decide to sell some assets, which would generate upward pressure on interest rates or depreciation pressure on the exchange rate. In this case, the current account deficit would not be sustainable by this definition. A large current account deficit alone need not engender these feedback relationships, however. If investors want to hold more assets of the country in question because growth there is strong, interest rates will not rise and the currency could appreciate. Finally, even if the trajectory is unsustainable, crisis is not inevitable. Feedback relationships can yield a smooth transition to a sustainable trajectory.

There are two points of view to any analysis of whether an external imbalance is sustainable: that of the borrower (the country in question) and that of the lender (the investor). The borrower cares about the implications for the domestic economy of both a trade deficit (which is a *flow* concept) and the net international investment position (which is a *stock* concept), because both represent future claims on the resources of the country that cannot be used for domestic consumption or investment. A trade deficit represents the value over a period of time of a country's borrowing on international markets, as a sovereign nation and/or as a collection of private market participants, to finance the excess of domestic spending over domestic production.[1] The net international investment position (NIIP) is the accumulation over time of trade deficits plus any additional borrowing needed to service (e.g., pay interest and dividends on)

---

1. The trade deficit can be expressed as the excess of total investment over total savings (public and private) or, alternatively, as the difference between production and expenditure. (For more on these approaches to analyzing the deficit, see chapters 3 and 8.) The point to remember is that if there is an external imbalance (a trade deficit), there is an internal imbalance (domestic demand exceeds production). In addition, whereas a trade deficit today means that resources are being transferred to the country from the rest of the world, in the future today's trade deficit and accumulated borrowing will have to be paid back—representing the future transfer of resources *back* to the rest of the world.

the NIIP. The sum of the trade deficit and net investment payments is the current account deficit.[2]

For the United States, the NIIP has been increasingly negative since the late 1980s (figure 10.1). This is a result not only of borrowing since 1980 to finance the persistent trade deficit but also of additional borrowing since 1997 to finance net investment payments on the negative NIIP.[3] From the standpoint of global investors, the US trade deficit represents the additional flow of US assets into their portfolio of wealth, and the negative NIIP represents the stock of US assets in their portfolio of wealth.

Borrower's Constraint

For a net borrower, a key sustainability relationship involves the accumulated stock of net international investments and the flow of trade deficits that accumulate to this stock.[4] A negative net international investment position cannot increase without bounds, since ultimately net investment payments on the negative position would use all the resources of the economy, leaving nothing for domestic consumption. From the standpoint of the domestic economy, the importance of the stock of foreign claims is best measured not by the NIIP itself but by the ratio of NIIP to GDP.

Even when the NIIP/GDP ratio reaches a constant value, net capital inflows (that is, net investment by foreigners) will continue, since GDP, which constitutes the wherewithal to service the obligations, increases as well. These net capital inflows represent the financing of the ongoing current account deficit. Thus, as GDP grows, capital inflows can continue, and the current account can remain in deficit and accumulate to a rising NIIP but a constant NIIP/GDP ratio.

The relationship between the current account and the NIIP/GDP ratio is affected primarily by two factors: the growth rate of GDP and the characteristics of the obligations. With a higher growth rate of the economy in the long run, servicing interest and principal on the NIIP accounts for a smaller share of future output, so it reduces domestic consumption and investment by less. Hence higher long-run growth allows a country to continue along its current trajectory of spending and saving (as measured by the current account deficit) longer than could a country with slower long-run growth.

---

2. For analytical purposes, I have left out unilateral transfers. As shown in figure 8.1, unilateral transfers have been increasing a bit over the years and hence they do affect the level of the deficit, but they are less important for understanding the dynamics of the current account deficit or the net international investment position.

3. For some time after the NIIP turned negative, the net investment payments were positive, because the rate of return on US investment abroad was greater than that on foreign investment in the United States. For more on this issue, see Stevens (1997).

4. This section and the next draw on Milesi-Ferretti and Razin (1996) and Sekiguchi (1997).

Figure 10.1 The stock and flow of US international investment, 1960-98

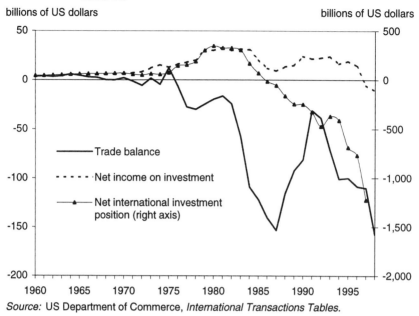

billions of US dollars   billions of US dollars

Trade balance

Net income on investment

Net international investment position (right axis)

Source: US Department of Commerce, *International Transactions Tables.*

As for the second factor, the lower the interest rate on debt obligations in the NIIP and the higher the share of equity obligations (which have contractual service requirements less strict than bank debt), the longer a country can run current account deficits, since the investment service likely is lower. In addition, the higher the share of obligations in the country's own currency, the less vulnerable the country is to exchange rate volatility. Hence a country that issues assets (that is, borrows) mostly in its own currency, at low interest rates, and with a high share of equity can continue along its trajectory of spending and saving for longer than could a country that borrows in currencies other than its own, at high interest rates, and using fixed-maturity debt.

At some point, investors will want to be repaid their principal, not just have their debt serviced. In theoretical terms, if all investors someday want to be repaid and there are no new investors, this means that a country that currently borrows will ultimately have to be a net lender—that is, run a trade surplus.[5] The present discounted value of the future years of

5. This simple presentation in the static world abstracts from many key features of the real world, including—most importantly—growth in wealth and the changing pattern of savers and investors around the world. The static presentation highlights the essential point, which is the link between investors' expectations for the future and the observable situation in the present.

trade surpluses must equal the outstanding net investment position. If the accumulation of *future* trade surpluses is too small, the principal plus interest will not be repaid—that is, the outstanding NIIP now is too large, which means that the current account deficits *now* also are too large.

When investors recognize that this situation might occur sometime in the future, they will not lend at current terms even today. Given this change in willingness to lend (that is, to invest in the borrowing country's assets), the borrower's interest rate rises as it tries to attract lenders, or its currency depreciates as existing lenders try to sell their investments, or investors simply are unwilling to lend at all (capital inflows cease)—or these tendencies occur in some combination. Once these forces are in motion, the current account deficit and the net international investment position have become unsustainable.

Empirical analysis can be used to determine the values for the ratio of NIIP to GDP and the ratio of current account to GDP (CA/GDP) at which investor sentiment can change and make the trajectory for the external accounts unsustainable. However, countries differ in their prospects for growth as well as in the maturity characteristics and currency composition of their debt. Other factors, such as global economic conditions, also will affect whether a country's external accounts are sustainable. Consequently, sustainability benchmarks derived from empirical analysis must be judged with caution and with an eye toward a country's particular situation as well as the prospects for the global economy.

Investor's Constraint

A country's obligations constitute assets in the wealth portfolios of global investors. Investors have their own portfolio constraints, which are similar to and related to the constraint on the NIIP/GDP ratio for the borrowing country. The highest possible share of a given global investor's portfolio allocated to the obligations of a given net borrowing country is 100 percent—though, of course, the share would likely settle at some lower level. Even if the portfolio share of one country's assets reaches some constant level, however, the value of those obligations could continue to rise as the value of global investors' portfolios increases.

How much lenders are willing to lend to residents of a country is a function of the risk-return profile of that borrower's assets relative to other assets as well as the investor's attitude toward risk and desire to diversify investments. Risk and return are codetermined by interest rates and currency valuations. The growth of the investor's home economy, the size of his or her global portfolio, and the available supply of alternative foreign investments also are important in determining how much of a country's assets the foreign investor wants. If the variability of the rate of return on a foreign investment increases—because of variability either in interest rates or in exchange rates—investment in that foreign asset generally declines. On the other hand, as the investor's country grows, the wealth portfolio grows, and lending to foreign countries increases.

The value of foreign financial assets added to the investor's portfolio must equal the value of financial assets offered by the borrowing country, which is its current account deficit. If the demand for these assets is too low (or if the current account deficits are too large), this means that the borrower's and the investors' desires do not match; there is a wedge between what the investors are willing to buy and what the borrower needs to sell. The investors may demand a higher return (interest rate), or may sell investments, causing the borrower's currency to depreciate. A higher interest rate will tend to slow the rate of growth of income and imports, and a depreciated currency will tend to shift relative prices in favor of domestic products and thus narrow the borrower's current account gap to bring it into line with what the investor is willing to finance. When these economic forces are set in motion, a current account deficit is revealed to be unsustainable.

Political Sustainability

There is a third dimension—political sustainability. It is clear that as a country's trade deficit grows large and differentially affects certain sectors, political activity on the trade agenda (on the part of both Congress and the administration) increases, often with the intent of protecting certain domestic markets.[6] The evidence suggests that political sustainability might break down far earlier than economic sustainability as measured from either the borrower's or the investor's perspective. In 1985, when the trade agenda was rife with protectionist legislation, the current account deficit was 3 percent of GDP; it would rise to 3.6 percent of GDP before the change in the value of the dollar worked through to change relative prices and trade flows. In 1998, although the current account deficit was a relatively smaller 2.6 percent of GDP and the US economy was growing rapidly with historically low unemployment and inflation rates, negotiations to liberalize trade remained at a standstill because the administration did not have "fast-track" negotiating authority. And in 1999, as several protectionist steel bills worked their way through Congress, steel imports were slapped with antidumping duties. What this political unsustainability might mean for the evolution of policy, particularly with regard to exchange rates, is discussed later in this chapter.

Sustainability and the Business Cycle

Finally, sustainability benchmarks can be applied over short-term or long-term time horizons. In most theoretical exercises that explore sustainability, it is usually the case that the key ratios of CA/GDP and NIIP/GDP are

6. See chapter 4 on how trade affects workers and chapter 6 on how trade policy affects trade and the trade balance, and the references cited there on the politics of trade policy.

always rising—that is, the trade deficit increases, the negative net investment position increases, and investment service payments increase until some critical value of the CA/GDP or NIIP/GDP ratio is reached. This is because rates of growth usually are assumed to be constant for the period of the exercise. As discussed in chapter 8, however, the US external balance has exhibited cyclical variation caused by changes in GDP growth on top of the trend widening of the deficit, negative NIIP, and net service payments; so the deficits and the CA/GDP ratio have not always been rising in the United States. Hence the trajectories of external balance that result from these modeling exercises and the application of sustainability benchmarks to those trajectories must be interpreted cautiously, since countries will experience business-cycle swings that generally are not reflected in the assumptions underlying the trajectories. In this regard, benchmarks for the CA/GDP or NIIP/GDP ratios have less value as point estimates than as indicators of when economic forces might start to build, which ultimately will drive the country back toward a sustainable path.

Empirical Criteria and Evidence of Sustainability for Industrial Countries

Given that real economic systems are in a state of constant change, evaluating sustainability implies comparing today's external flows and net international investment position to empirical observations for the sustainability benchmarks. There is a rich sample of sustainability crises that offer empirical observations (Goldstein, Kaminsky, and Reinhart, forthcoming). While most of these events pertain to low- and middle-income countries, there have been episodes of financial-market instability and questions of current account sustainability for some high-income countries as well. From these episodes, empirical regularities might point to sustainability benchmarks for industrial countries that can be applied to US data.

In data from the 1980s and 1990s for 10 industrial countries, we can pick out 17 episodes in which a trend widening of a current account deficit was reversed.[7] The reasons for these reversals are not addressed, however, so they are not necessarily all sustainability episodes. With the outliers excluded, the average CA/GDP ratio was –4.2 percent when the current ac-

---

7. The countries and years of the episodes are: Australia, 1986 and 1995; Canada, 1981 and 1991; Finland, 1983 and 1991; Italy, 1981 and 1992; Norway, 1986; New Zealand, 1984 and 1996; Spain, 1981 and 1991; Sweden, 1982 and 1992; United Kingdom, 1989; and United States, 1987. I have selected the 1980s and 1990s observation time frame because financial markets play the key role in sustainability (see chapter 9), and these markets have changed dramatically in the past 20 years. For reference, however, in 1971, when the dollar was devalued 10 percent in the Smithsonian Agreement realignments, the current account was headed for –$5.8 billion or 0.5 percent of GDP in 1972. In 1978, when the dollar began a bout of depreciation, the current account deficit was $15.1 billion or about 0.7 percent of GDP. (The merchandise trade deficit and its share of GDP were twice these magnitudes—thus pointing again to the potential impact of political sustainability.)

**Table 10.1 Selected industrial countries: Institutional investors'
holdings of securities issued by nonresidents**
(percentage of total assets)

	1980	1988	1990	1991	1992	1993	1994	1995
Pension funds								
United States	0.7	2.7	4.2	4.1	4.6	5.7	n.a.	n.a.
Japan	0.5	6.3	7.2	8.4	8.4	9.0	n.a.	n.a.
Germany	n.a.	3.8	4.5	4.5	4.3	4.5	5.0	n.a.
United Kingdom	7.9	16.3	17.8	20.6	19.5	20.0	19.8	19.8
Canada	4.9	5.9	6.4	8.6	10.2	11.6	12.9	14.2
Mutual funds								
United States	n.a.	n.a.	6.6	n.a.	10.1	n.a.	n.a.	n.a.
Japan	n.a.	9.1	7.9	13.0	9.9	n.a.	n.a.	n.a.
Germany	n.a.	n.a.	n.a.	n.a.	n.a.	24.8	20.3	20.2
United Kingdom	17.9	33.0	31.0	34.3	35.2	35.8	36.4	34.5
Canada	19.9	19.4	17.5	16.1	17.0	20.0	24.0	24.6

n.a. = not available

Source: IMF, *International Capital Markets* (September 1998).

count started to narrow. Throughout these episodes, the NIIP/GDP ratio
continued to climb, so this criterion does not appear to be the one that
triggers the economic forces leading to the change in the current account
trajectory.

For a sustainability benchmark based on the share of foreign assets in a
global portfolio—the investor's constraint—there are fewer empirical examples. In general, market participants put the majority of their wealth
into financial assets from their own country,[8] although for the international financial markets as a whole, there is a clear preference for dollar-
denominated assets (though not all of these are claims on US resources)
(see table 2.1). In individual portfolios, the share of wealth invested in
securities issued by nonresidents has risen over time, particularly with
the increasing globalization of finance and financial institutions. In some
countries mutual funds invest about one-third of their portfolio of assets
in nonresident securities, but in other countries and in other investment
funds the share is much lower (table 10.1).

Applying the Analytical Framework and
Empirical Benchmarks to US Data

We now have an analytical foundation for assessing sustainability and
some empirical benchmarks from previous US experience as well as from

8. See Lewis (1999) for a review of the literature on home bias.

Table 10.2 Exogenous variables and sustainability framework

	1999	2000	High performance	Business as usual
			2001-10	
US real GDP (percentage)[a]	3.3	2.2	2.7	2.1
World real GDP (percentage)[a]	2.3	3.4	5.0	3.2
Export income elasticity	1.0	1.0	1.0	1.0
Import income elasticity	1.7	1.7	1.7	1.7
Interest rate (percentage)	4.0	4.0	4.0	4.0
Inflation rate (percentage)	2.0	2.0	2.0	2.0

a. Forecast for 1999 and 2000 from IMF, *World Economic Outlook* (May 1999). Estimates for 2001-10 from OECD (1997). Other data are author's estimates.

Sustainability framework

$EX = EX(t-1) * (1 + Y_w * E_{ex}/100 + (NEU - NEU(t-1)) / NEU(t-1))$
$IM = IM(t-1) * (1 + Y_{us} * E_{im}/100 - (NEU - NEU(t-1)) / NEU(t-1))$
$TB = EX - IM$
$CA = TB + NIIP(t-1) * r$
$NIIP = NIIP(t-1) + CA = NIIP(t-1) + NIIP(t-1) * r + TB$

Where:
EX = exports
IM = imports
TB = trade balance
CA = current account
NIIP = net international investment position
E_{ex} = export income elasticity
E_{im} = import income elasticity
NEU = nominal effective exchange rate index
Y_w = world growth (nominal)
Y_{us} = US growth (nominal)
r = nominal interest rate

Note: $(t-1)$ indicates a lag.

other industrial countries. The benchmarks can be applied to US data to assess the sustainability of US external dynamics, now and in the future. The sustainability exercise has the following inputs: the analytical framework; data on exports, imports, current account, and NIIP; empirical values for critical parameters, such as the marginal propensity to import and export, which are key drivers of the trade balance; and trajectories for key variables such as forecasts for near-term GDP growth and estimates of long-term potential growth of GDP and the world interest rate and inflation rate (table 10.2).

The sustainability framework is a set of simple equations. Assumptions about the growth rate of US and foreign income and the exchange rate along with the export and import income elasticities generate trajectories for exports, imports, and the trade balance.[9] The current account equation adds up the trade balance and service payments on the NIIP, using an assumption for the nominal interest rate. The NIIP equation accumulates the current account deficits.

The near-term growth rates are taken from the IMF's May 1999 *World Economic Outlook*. Changes in the near-term outlook have been significant (as discussed in chapter 8) and have an important impact on the near-term assessment of sustainability. Estimating the long-term rate of growth of potential is substantially more complex. The OECD has undertaken an extensive exercise to examine two alternative scenarios for the world to 2010 and on to 2020: a "business-as-usual" scenario, leading to relatively low growth in the United States (2.1 percent) and worldwide (3.2 percent), and a "high-performance" scenario, leading to more rapid growth in the United States (2.7 percent) and worldwide (5 percent). As described by the OECD:

> The "business as usual" case assumes a continuation in current productivity trends with limited progress in trade and investment liberalization, structural reforms, and budgetary control.

> The "high-performance" case assumes more favourable trends in international liberalization of trade and investment policies, accompanied by a stepping up of the pace of structural reforms, including regulatory and budgetary reforms, and a stable macroeconomic environment.[10]

Three snapshots in time on the trajectories are presented in table 10.3: the near horizon to 2000, a medium-term horizon to 2005, and the long-term horizon to 2010. The near-term snapshot focuses on whether the consequences for global growth of the 1997-98 financial turmoil could precipitate a sustainability episode as the US economy continues to grow rapidly and the rest of the world grows slowly. The medium-term snapshot asks whether the rebound in global economic activity as the financial turmoil subsides and growth resumes, along with the projected slowing in the growth rate of the US economy, keeps the United States on a sustainable track. Finally, the question for 2010 is, once the US and global economies reach their estimated rates of growth of potential output, will the US external balance be sustainable given estimated parameters of export and import income elasticity? The structural changes underpin-

---

9. This is a simplified version of the income and relative price model discussed in chapter 8. However, in no way should the trajectories be viewed as forecasts, since I make two key simplifications. The first is to assume that all prices are rising at the same rate—2 percent. In fact, as discussed in chapters 5 and 7, import and export prices have been rising more slowly (or even falling) compared to broader measures of inflation, such as the GDP deflator. The second is to assume full pass-through of an exchange rate change into relative prices and an immediate response on the part of trade flows—i.e., no J-curve. (See chapter 7 for more discussion of exchange rate pass-through, and chapter 9 for a discussion of the J-curve.)

10. *OECD Economic Outlook* (December 1997, 42). For more substantive discussion, see also OECD (1997). See chapter 5 for a discussion of how globalization raises US productivity growth, which supports the OECD's linking of trade liberalization and productivity growth.

Table 10.3 Alternative scenarios

	Near horizon: 2000	Medium horizon: 2005 High performance	Medium horizon: 2005 Business as usual	Long horizon: 2010 High performance	Long horizon: 2010 Business as usual
Base case scenario, import elasticity 1.7, export elasticity 1.0					
Trade balance	-248.5	-432.7	-463.0	-730.7	-796.7
Current account (billions of US dollars)	-316.6	-583.3	-616.0	-1,030.0	-1,108.5
Current account (share of GDP, percentage)	-3.4	-5.0	-5.4	-7.0	-8.0
NIIP (billions of US dollars)	-2,020.4	-4,347.6	-4,440.3	-8,514.3	-8,903.0
NIIP (share of GDP, percentage)	-21.8	-37.3	-39.2	-58.0	-64.2
FEER scenario, US dollar weakens by about 25 percentage points					
Trade balance (billions of US dollars)	-96.9	-220.2	-267.8	-432.6	-545.2
Current account (billions of US dollars)	-166.6	-335.1	-386.3	-635.8	-768.3
Current account (share of GDP, percentage)	-1.8	-2.9	-3.4	-4.3	-5.5
NIIP (billions of US dollars)	-1,908.5	-3,206.9	-3,350.1	-5,717.2	-6,347.0
NIIP (share of GDP, percentage)	-20.6	-27.5	-29.5	-38.9	-45.8
Service export scenario, import elasticity 1.7, export elasticity 1.3					
Trade balance (billions of US dollars)	-219.8	-241.6	-322.3	-229.2	-471.5
Current account (billions of US dollars)	-287.5	-373.7	-460.2	-442.1	-720.5
Current account (share of GDP, percentage)	-3.1	-3.2	-4.1	-3.0	-5.2
NIIP (billions of US dollars)	-1,979.2	-3,676.7	-3,906.1	-5,764.5	-6,945.6
NIIP (share of GDP, percentage)	-21.3	-31.5	-34.4	-39.3	-50.1

NIIP = net international investment position
FEER = fundamental equilibrium exchange rate

Sources: Forecast for 2000 from IMF, *World Economic Outlook* (May 1999). Estimates for 2002-10 from OECD (1997). Other data are author's estimates.

ning the high-performance scenario, for the world and for the United States, will have a critical impact on whether the US external accounts are sustainable in the long run.

Base Case

In the base case, GDP growth for the United States remains robust through 1999 at 3.3 percent, whereas world growth, at 2.3 percent, remains severely affected by the financial crises of 1997-98. As we move into 2000, world growth picks up some (3.4 percent), whereas US growth is projected to slow a bit (2.2 percent). Out to 2010, growth rates for the United States and the world are the same as in the two OECD scenarios (discussed above). In the base case, the exchange value of the dollar remains at its trade-weighted value in late 1998 and early 1999 (about 120 on the IMF's nominal effective exchange-rate index; 1995 = 100).

The base case suggests that the US current account is on a trajectory that is sustainable for about three years, with a CA/GDP ratio of about −3 per-

Figure10.2 Growth rates and current account: Scenarios to 2010

A. Low-growth scenario

percentage of GDP

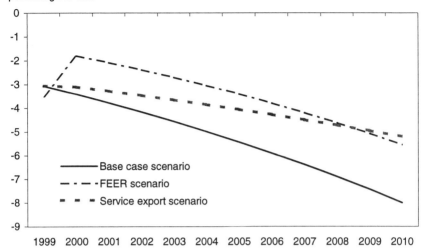

B. High-growth scenario

percentage of GDP

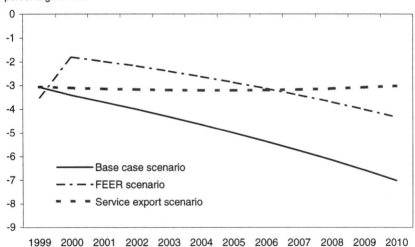

cent through 2000, increasing to about −3.8 percent by the end of 2001 (table 10.3 and figure 10.2). In 2000, as growth resumes abroad and slows to a sustainable pace in the United States, the pace of deterioration in the CA/GDP ratio briefly slows. Thus, if the CA/GDP ratio is sustained through 1999, it can be sustained for another year after that. Moreover, even at −4.2 percent (at the end of 2002 in the business-as-usual case) the CA/GDP ratio is at the average turning point for other industrial countries. Given the characteristics of US net international obligations (as I argue below), the sustainability benchmark for the US CA/GDP ratio is likely to be a larger figure than that for other industrial countries. All of this suggests that the trajectory could be sustained for two or three more years.

On the other hand, the CA/GDP ratio was only −3.0 percent in 1985 (headed toward 3.6 percent two years later), when trade policy activity was at a peak and when government intervention and market sentiment caused the dollar to reverse its appreciation. And, as indicated in one of the quotations at the beginning of the chapter, some market participants are already wondering about sustainability when the CA/GDP is less than −3 percent. Thus, the next few years may highlight a tension between economic sustainability, as measured by the borrower's constraint, and political sustainability, in which market sentiment can be a key factor.[11]

By 2005, the effect of the asymmetry in the income elasticity of imports and exports starts to widen the trade deficit, regardless of the estimate for GDP growth. In 2005, the CA/GDP ratios of –5.0 percent in the high-performance scenario and –5.4 percent in the business-as-usual scenario are beyond any in US experience, and exceed the average of the other industrial countries' episodes, although they are still within the bounds of industrial-country experience. The value of the current account deficit, though, is about $600 billion, well outside any country's experience. While the negative NIIP grows to more than $4 trillion in this scenario, this is less than the *national* debt in 1998 and only about 40 percent of GDP, and the net investment payments account for a quite small 1 percent transfer of resources abroad.

Nevertheless, the trajectory for the external accounts is set by 2005 and plays out to 2010 and beyond. At this horizon, the buildup of the negative NIIP (the consequence of persistent trade and current account deficits) and the income asymmetry drive the dynamics of the current account and of sustainability. By 2010 the CA/GDP ratio is beyond any empirical trigger suggested by the experiences of the industrial countries. The current account deficit exceeds $1 trillion. The NIIP/GDP ratio grows, although it is still not all that large, and the net investment payments on the NIIP amount to approximately 2 percent of GDP.

Thus far the discussion has focused on the borrower's constraints. What about the investor's constraints? By 2005, foreign investors would be asked to incorporate about $2.4 trillion more of US assets into their port-

---

11. The role of market sentiment and current account data in precipitating crises through self-fulfilling prophecy is a large field with much ongoing research. A quick overview of the complex relationship between current account news and movements of the exchange rate can be found in Levich (1998, 172-75); see also Krugman (1985).

folios, and by 2010, about $4 trillion more.[12] Will foreign investors be willing to add this much to their global portfolios? To put this figure into perspective, consider that the value in 1997 of net financial wealth in six of the largest industrial countries (not including the United States) was about $25 trillion.[13] Given the growth this collective portfolio itself would undergo from 1997 to 2005, the amount to be added by 2005 would represent less than 10 percent of the total.

For the period from 2005 to 2010, the value of US assets to be added to the global financial marketplace through the US current account deficit would be some $4.5 trillion. The value of wealth in these six industrial countries would grow by about $10 trillion. The global portfolios of the largest industrial countries would thus have to acquire significantly more US assets by 2010. However, by then net wealth accumulation in other countries around the world probably would be significant, and investors in those countries would probably want to invest in US assets.

Indeed, the six countries accounted for about half of global GDP (excluding the United States) in 1997, and growth and wealth accumulation in many countries other than the six presumably will increasingly dominate the financial landscape. Moreover, as noted in the discussion of home bias, there is substantial room for all investors to increase their share of nondomestic assets. But it is impossible to know whether investors' preferences for US assets over their own countries' assets will coincide with increased availability of US assets. All told, this calculation for the investor constraint alongside the borrower constraint supports the notion that the US current account is sustainable for at least two or three more years, or even longer as judged by the investors' constraint. These somewhat different horizons set up a possible tension between the two criteria—borrower and investor—of economic sustainability.[14]

---

12. The dollar value is the additional assets sold abroad represented by the accumulated current account deficits; it is the net capital flow. Of course, US investors will purchase foreign assets during the time period, and that capital flow will also need to be financed.

13. The six countries for which detailed data are available are Canada, Germany, France, Italy, Japan, and the United Kingdom. This calculation assumes an average share of net financial wealth to nominal household income of 250 percent (OECD 1998b, annex table 58, p. 249); assumes that personal income is 75 percent of GDP (personal income is 84 percent of GDP in the United States, so this figure is conservative); and calculates nominal GDP in dollar terms using period average nominal exchange rates. Growth in the portfolio uses this same method and the rate of growth of nominal GDP in table 10.2, averaging between the high-growth and low-growth scenarios where appropriate.

14. These trajectories assume that the import and export elasticities are estimated with certainty and that the simple framework is a correct model of economic relationships. In fact, model and parameter uncertainty are important issues that can completely change the outlook for US external balances over long-term trajectories. See Mann (1991) for further discussion.

Figure 10.3　Share of liabilities to foreigners payable in dollars, reported by banks, 1983-96

percentage

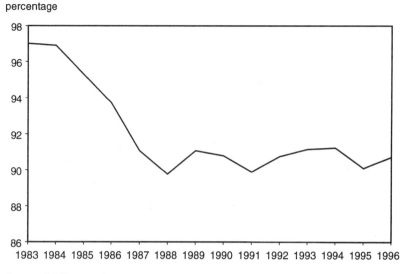

Source: US Treasury Department, *Treasury Bulletin.*

Is the United States Special?

The results for the base case suggest that the CA/GDP ratio for the United States could test the limits of sustainability in two or three years, at least from the viewpoint of the borrower's constraint. However, in some key respects the United States is special in international financial markets, and the sustainability benchmarks for the borrower's constraint determined both from our 1985 (and earlier) experience and from the experiences of other industrial countries may not be applicable.

First, much of US international borrowing is in dollars, although the share has fallen somewhat in recent years (figure 10.3). Hence the most explosive difficulty that some countries have faced in sustainability crises—the inability to exchange the domestic currency for the currency in which it needs to make payments—will not be an issue for the United States. However, if investors have reached the desired share of dollars in their portfolios, then the United States could find itself having to offer higher interest rates to attract investors. This would imply that the current account has become unsustainable, but not that a crisis is imminent.

Second, US assets sold to finance the external deficit have contractual characteristics that make them relatively more stable in the case of a sudden change in investor confidence. For example, bank credit lines and short-term bills are relatively unstable; if investors lose confidence, they let the short-term credits mature and then refuse to roll them over into new debt. For the United States, about 75 percent of foreign private investment is in longer-term, more stable investments: direct investment, bonds with maturities greater than one year, and stocks.[15] Should investors lose confidence in the US economy, the value of these assets would decline (in particular, the stock market value and bond prices would fall as foreign investors sold some of the assets), but the consequences of price movements would be less serious, particularly in the short term, than if investors simply will not roll over credits.[16] To be sure, a fall in the stock market and bond prices would hurt the United States; consumer confidence would be shaken, consumption would decline, and higher interest rates and financial market volatility would have a negative effect on business investment. However, these are manifestations of the economy's adjusting to a situation of external unsustainability and do not necessarily imply a crisis.[17]

On the other hand, an important component of the financing of the US external balance in recent years has been foreign purchases of US Treasury securities, apparently predominantly by a relatively small set of countries (figure 10.4). Is the US external position more likely to become unsustainable because of this concentrated lending and holding of US Treasury securities? In 1998, 36 percent of US government securities were held abroad, up from 25 percent just three years before. Limited data suggest that Japan is a large shareholder, holding perhaps one-fifth of the US government securities held abroad. These figures should be interpreted with care, however. Foreign investors are a diverse group, and there is no reason to suppose that all Japanese investors have the same risk-return profile. Moreover, the data are collected according to the location of the investor's agent; an investor from Singapore could well purchase US Treasury securities through a Japanese agent.

But suppose all the "Japanese" net purchasers did have the same risk and return preferences. And suppose they all decided to sell their US government securities at once because of a systematic "Japan-US" shock that raised the riskiness of holding US government securities or raised the returns on Japanese securities.[18] There could be an upward pressure on

---

15. See chapter 3 for more detail on the composition of the capital account. For additional discussion of the implication of the composition of external credit for the stability of external finance, see Claessens and Gooptu (1993).

16. It is one thing to have to pay more for credit, and another to be unable to get credit at any price.

17. Proper monetary policy can smooth the adjustment path if unstable reactions set in. Examples include the injection of central bank credit in September 1987 when stock markets around the world were collapsing and the quick three-step reduction in the US federal funds rate in the fall of 1998 after the Russian default on debt caused liquidity in US financial markets to dry up.

18. Concern over this possibility was voiced in early 1999 (and numerous other occasions) as interest rates on Japanese securities were rising on account of the expected need to finance the fiscal programs in Japan.

Figure 10.4 Foreign holdings of US Treasury securities, 1984-98

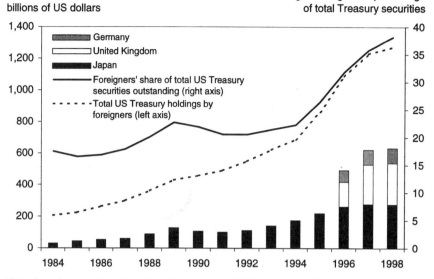

Note: Data for countries other than Japan before 1995 are not available.

Source: US Treasury Department, *Treasury Bulletin.*

interest rates on US government securities or a downward pressure on the exchange value of the dollar. But would these pressures lead to a sustained change in the value of US securities or to an external sustainability crisis? These outcomes are unlikely, because the domestic and global markets for these securities are the most mature in the world, and the rest of the domestic and international investor body remains available to buy the securities, which likely would be bargain priced under such circumstances. The diversity of investors around the world and the importance of the United States to the global trade and financial markets are stabilizing features that make the United States special.

Looked at from yet a third perspective, net purchases of US government securities have, at times, been inordinately important as a balancing investment to the trade deficit, particularly in the 1995-97 period (figure 10.5). Some view foreign investment in US government securities as a mercantilist way of keeping the dollar exchange rate from depreciating and facilitating the adjustment in the US external balance (e.g., Preeg 1998). In this vein, some argue that while foreigners are willing to buy US assets, they are not willing to buy US goods and services for fear of creating an environment of greater competition and choice in their domestic economies that is disruptive to sheltered firms and sectors. While these arguments have merit, the evidence from 1998 shows that, on balance, foreign official investors sold US government assets from their portfolios.

Figure 10.5   Net US assets: Capital flows, 1980-98

billions of US dollars

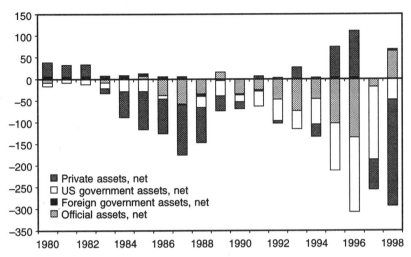

Note: Positive numbers represent net outflow, and negative numbers represent net inflow.
Sources: Bureau of Economic Analysis, *International Transactions Tables*, Historical Data;
US Department of Commerce, *Survey of Current Business.*

Not only has no US sustainability crisis ensued, but in fact the dollar continued to appreciate.

On the whole, investors around the world realize that relatively safe and high-yielding US investments are the best place to park their wealth right now given the financial turbulence in Asia and the uncertain currency marriage in Europe. However, there will come a time when US assets are no longer as attractive, either because returns in the United States are falling and/or because returns abroad are rising. At that point investors will choose other assets, the cost of financing the US external deficit will rise, the dollar may depreciate and/or US income growth will slow, and/or policies to change the structure of US and global trade flows will work to close the external deficit and put it on a sustainable path. Such changes will mean that the external balance has become unsustainable; they would not have to engender a crisis. Yet, to the extent that investors continue to augment—and perhaps to overweight—their portfolios with US assets rather than to buy foreign assets, an abrupt change could occur in the value of the dollar when their sentiment does change.

Ways to Achieve Sustainability

In the base case scenario, the constellation of economic growth, relative prices, and trade structure yields trajectories for the external accounts that will be unsustainable in two or three years and certainly are unsustainable in the long term. What alternative constellations would make the external trajectories sustainable? The economic forces outlined in the analytical framework point to how an economy might respond. Recall that a sustainability episode can occur when investors are no longer willing to invest in a country by purchasing its assets. In the context of the framework, this is because the investors fear that they will not receive the expected rate of return—or, more radically, they fear for their principal.

Under such a scenario, the dearth of investors for a given flow of obligations entering the international marketplace leads to economic reactions that can move the economy back toward a sustainable path. First, the interest rate on the obligations would increase, simply from the forces of supply and demand. The increase should help to slow the economy and narrow the trade gap, and thus tend to reduce the need for investor credit. So long as the increase in interest rates does not raise the net investment payments faster than the trade account narrows, this response would constitute an equilibrating mechanism that gets the economy back on a sustainable track.

Second, with fewer investors, the exchange value of the currency should tend to depreciate, which would change relative prices of exports and imports to domestic goods and services, which in turn would tend to narrow the trade gap and slow the flow of US assets into the international marketplace. So long as the exchange rate change does not raise the domestic currency value of investment payments and of the external stock of obligations faster than the trade account narrows, this too would constitute an equilibrating response. Because the bulk of US obligations are denominated in dollars, a depreciation of the dollar almost surely would be an equilibrating force that would put the external accounts onto a sustainable path. Or would it?

Dollar Depreciation: Medium-Term But Not Long-Term Sustainability

Calculating what value of the dollar might yield a sustainable trajectory for the current account is a difficult task, since the two are endogenous; that is, the sustainable value of the dollar depends on the sustainable value of the current account deficit. Moreover, both of these have important effects on growth and trade in the rest of the world. Wren-Lewis and Driver (1998) offer one set of calculations for the dollar that depend in turn on calculations for the current account from a detailed global model.

Wren-Lewis and Driver calculate a fundamental equilibrium exchange rate (FEER) value of the dollar for 2000 of about 95 yen/dollar and about 1.3 dollars/euro. Compared with the exchange rates that prevailed at the beginning of 1999, this suggests that the dollar would need to depreciate some 25 percent against the yen and 10 percent against the euro. On the basis of broader trade weights, 25 percent is a good ballpark figure for how much the dollar would have to depreciate to reach its fundamental equilibrium exchange rate. Suppose this depreciation took place immediately (1999), and the dollar stayed at this lower level for the duration of the scenario. The effects of this depreciation over the next few years would be dramatic; indeed, the simple framework overemphasizes the speed with which the current account would respond.[19] The key point, however, is that over the longer term, dollar depreciation would only postpone the sustainability problem, not eliminate it (see table 10.3 and figure 10.2).

Suppose, then, that the dollar did depreciate some 25 percent. The current account deficit would be cut in half, with the effect on the trade deficit even larger. The CA/GDP ratio would narrow to less than –2.0 percent in the next two or three years. But after about five years, the dramatic effect begins to diminish as the trade account and current account widen again because of the income asymmetry—even though US growth is slowing and world growth is rebounding. Nevertheless, because the effect of the depreciation is so great, even five years out its effect remains on the *level* of the current account as well as the CA/GDP ratio. The depreciation puts this indicator comfortably within the range of previous US experience at –2.9 percent in the high-performance scenario and –3.4 percent in the business-as-usual scenario.

Over the long term, the dynamics of the income asymmetry take over and are augmented by the net investment-service payments, and the CA/GDP ratio rises to the range of -4.3 to -5.5 percent. The worsening of the current account deficit kicks in sooner than might be expected on the basis of the historical relationship between exchange rate changes and the trade balance. A change in the value of the dollar affects only the trajectory of exports and imports; it does not directly affect net investment-service payments, which are a rising fraction of the current account deficit. Consequently, the salutary effects on the current account of a depreciation of the dollar are smaller and shorter lived than they have been in the past, because the negative NIIP of the United States is so large. If everything else remained unchanged, the 25 percent depreciation of the dollar would buy about five more years of sustainability for the CA/GDP ratio in comparison to the base case.

However, the FEER scenario raises another issue that is particularly relevant in the current environment of a robust US economy. With a 25 percent depreciation, the shrinking of the US trade deficit would add back about $150 billion dollars of spending to US goods and services within a year or two. The US economy would be hard pressed to generate approximately 1.7 percent more of GDP without running into even greater constraints on resource usage, particularly in the labor markets.[20]

---

19. In the simple framework, with full pass-through and no J-curve, the effects of a depreciation are observed immediately, instead of taking one or two years to play out.

20. See chapter 5 for a discussion of the inflation-output relationship and how it has been affected by exchange rate movements and global forces.

In addition to the potential for wage inflation, the depreciation of the dollar would tend to raise import prices, with domestic prices likely to follow, and then monetary tightening as the likely policy response. As discussed in chapter 5, the appreciation of the dollar has played an important role in keeping US inflation low. Since 1996 the declines in import prices associated with the appreciating dollar have cut about 1.8 percentage points off CPI inflation. A depreciation of the dollar of some 25 percent could ultimately pass through to raise the inflation rate, both directly by raising input costs and prices of imported products and indirectly by allowing US producers to gain pricing power and raise prices. Moreover, a rise in domestic inflation would tend to push up wages beyond productivity growth, as workers in this unprecedentedly tight labor market have greater ability to bargain. Rising inflation (or the threat of rising inflation) is a key signal for monetary policymakers to respond by raising interest rates, which tends to slow domestic economic activity as borrowing costs rise. Although monetary authorities in this case would not intend to initiate a recession, monetary policy is not a precise instrument. On some previous occasions (see figure 5.1) rising inflation has presaged slower GDP growth, and indeed, sometimes recessions. A significant depreciation of the dollar thus could set in motion *internal* forces that unhappily could lead to the slowing of US growth while at the same time yielding the positive outcome of enabling the economy to skirt the *external* sustainability criteria.

Structural Change to Achieve a Sustainable Trajectory

Underlying both the base case and the FEER scenario are the asymmetric income elasticities of trade (see chapter 8) and the estimates of the rate of growth of potential output in the United States and the world (for the United States, see further discussion in chapter 5). Changes in these parameters and estimates could yield a sustainable current account position both in the medium term and the long term without any change in the value of the dollar from its current level.

What if the income elasticity of exports were to increase from 1.0 to 1.3 on account of economic development abroad, liberalization of international markets, and a rising share of service-sector trade in US exports?[21] If the rest of the world proceeded along the "business-as-usual" path, this

---

21. The increasing share of services in US exports is discussed in chapter 3, the implications of service-sector liberalization for export growth in chapter 6, and how trade flows change when income changes in chapter 8. The export-income elasticity estimate of 1.3 is a weighted average (goods and services weights at 0.7 and 0.3, respectively—see table 3.3) of 1.0 for goods (taken from long-period regressions shown in table 8.2) and 1.9 for services (see table 8.1 and Wren-Lewis and Driver 1998, appendix C).

change in the value of the export elasticity would slow the widening of the current account deficit, but not otherwise substantially change its trajectory from the base case scenario (figure 10.2).

However, if the world embarked upon a path of trade liberalization, particularly in the services sector, this would likely be accompanied by the high-performance scenario for US and world growth. Indeed, service-sector deregulation and liberalization specifically (in both home and global markets) are among the types of reforms that underpin the higher productivity growth embodied in the high-performance estimates by the OECD. (Labor market reforms are another key element, particularly abroad.) The US experience in the relationship between globalization and productivity growth (discussed in chapter 5) bolsters the underpinnings of the OECD high-performance scenario.

Structural change in the export elasticity along with high-performance growth in the United States and the rest of the world makes the US external accounts sustainable and keeps them on a sustainable trajectory. The CA/GDP ratio remains around 3 percent throughout the trajectory, and indeed, the ratio starts to narrow toward 2010. In sum, structural change in both the United States and the rest of the world would put the US external balances on a sustainable trajectory. What is clear from the low- vs. high-growth scenarios, however, is that the United States cannot be alone in making the reforms. Because liberalization of trade and of domestic markets go hand-in-hand, particularly for the services sector, the United States should move quickly to launch and encourage wide participation in a new trade round.

Political Sustainability and Changes in the Value of the Dollar

The scenarios discussed above address questions of economic sustainability. From the standpoint of political sustainability, however, we might already have reached the limit of the trade deficit, given the four or five bills proposed recently in Congress to address specific sectors (although, as noted in chapter 6, this is a small number of trade bills compared to 1985). Trade surges also might generate a revival of Section 201 or Section 301 trade remedies. US policymakers might respond to trade pressures and either "talk the dollar down" or, as in 1985, the G-7 group of industrial nations could use concerted intervention to help the dollar depreciate (Funabashi, 1989).[22]

---

22. It should be noted, however, that in contrast to 1985, as of June 1999, policymakers in Euroland were talking the euro down and Japanese policymakers were engaging in foreign exchange market intervention to keep the yen from appreciating—in effect the opposite of the 1985 activity.

The FEER scenario shows that a change in the exchange value of the dollar is a potent weapon for changing the trajectory of the trade and current account deficits in the next five years or so. Although this could tempt policymakers under political pressure to use dollar rhetoric and perhaps market intervention to change the value of the dollar, the trajectories also make clear that changes in structural parameters associated with economic reforms at home and abroad will lead to a long-term sustainable external balance for the United States, given the expectation for future growth. A once-and-for-all change in the value of the dollar alone does not yield long-term sustainability.[23]

Policymakers can consider the quick fix of dollar depreciation, which narrows the deficits now but does not change the economic fundamentals. But they must be wary of the potential inflationary consequences of their action and the likely monetary policy response. Moreover, they should address the structural changes—both abroad in efforts to liberalize trade and internally in efforts to increase household savings and prepare the workforce—to put the sustainability of the US external balance on a more solid footing for the long term.

Implications of the Euro for Sustainability

The introduction of the euro constitutes a major change in the currency landscape and could conceivably press the US external deficit more rapidly toward unsustainable benchmarks. The new currency influences the sustainability benchmarks primarily on the investors' side. The availability of this new foreign asset should reduce the demand for investments in US assets once the market for euro-denominated assets is larger and more liquid than the markets for assets denominated in the national European currencies that it replaces. Although all the existing debt issued in the Euroland currencies has been translated into euro obligations, the share of euro-denominated instruments accounts for only a bit more than one-fourth of the global bond market against nearly one-half accounted for by dollar-denominated assets and one-fifth by yen-denominated assets (see table 2.1). Therefore, much more issuance of new instruments in euro is necessary.

At what point will the euro challenge the dollar as a financial asset? It depends on the risk-return profile of the euro instruments that represent claims on Euroland assets relative to that of dollar instruments that rep-

---

23. A slow but steady depreciation of the dollar might close the trade gap over a very long term, although there is some question about whether it could close the current account gap because of rising net investment payments. There is no evidence that financial markets would enable this path, nor that policymakers would (or could) enforce this regime. See the analyses and caveats presented in Marris (1985, 114-117) and Krugman (1985) regarding this issue in 1985, the last time the current account gap was so large.

resent claims on US assets. Risk and return depend on liquidity (itself important) as well as on the rate of growth in the market generating the claims. Suppose the euro financial market develops rapidly, so that it is a deeper and more liquid market than any of its predecessor markets (Bergsten 1997). Suppose, too, that Euroland begins a rebound in growth over the next two years. During this same period, the US external deficits could be widening, absorbing the tail end of the cyclical effect of continued robust US growth, the slowdowns in Asia and Latin America, and the appreciation of the dollar. Moreover, the longer-term sustainability benchmarks would be just around the corner and clear for all to see. Thus the shift in international investors' preferences toward holding a greater share of euro in their portfolios could occur about the same time that the sustainability criteria from the borrower's side began to put the bite on the United States. The dollar would get a push toward depreciation from both sides of the sustainability criteria (borrower and investor), and a push could become a rout unless the structural changes discussed in this volume are in train and help to limit the fall.

Conclusion

■ The global financial crises and the robust US economy together have moved the US external accounts toward unsustainable territory. Yet because the United States is both special and a critical participant in the international markets, our robust domestic demand can continue to support the resumption of global growth for two or three more years. Given the structural asymmetries in the components of the US external balance and political and market sensitivities toward ever-increasing trade deficits, however, the economic forces leading to a narrowing of the trade imbalance are likely to build within and certainly beyond that time frame.

■ Structural changes that are in train and that could be furthered by policy initiatives could make a significant difference to this picture and have a lasting impact on the trajectories for US trade and external accounts. On the domestic side, the United States must pursue a number of structural changes, including an increase in the household savings rate and an improvement in worker preparedness for current and future jobs. On the export side, economic development abroad and liberalization of the service sector through active trade negotiations would yield an increasing share of services in total exports that would significantly change the prospects for US external balances. But the United States cannot act alone; liberalization and productivity-enhancing policies must be implemented abroad as well. High performance at home and abroad enhances not only the long-term economic prospects of both the United States and the world but also the sustainability of the US external accounts.

■ A significant depreciation of the dollar would put the external accounts back into sustainable territory for the near and medium terms, but not on a sustainable trajectory for the long term. While the impact of a significant depreciation is dramatic, without structural changes and more robust productivity growth a depreciation of the dollar continues the cycle whereby a depreciation narrows the external balances but is followed by renewed widening of the imbalances as structural instabilities and net investment payments take hold. This precipitates another dollar depreciation, and so on. The dollar has been on this roller coaster since the breakdown of the Bretton Woods system, but since the NIIP is now negative, the ride could get wilder.

■ From a political standpoint, congressional and administration activity on the trade front suggests that sustainability benchmarks have already been breached. This poses an unhappy dilemma for policymakers: capitulate with specific, ineffective protections (see chapter 6) or try to narrow the deficit quickly with a change in the value of the dollar. Orchestrating a dollar depreciation would reduce political pressures but would not improve the structural determinants of the external accounts. Moreover, it would likely generate inflationary pressure and a monetary policy response that would slow US economic growth.

■ For a whole host of reasons, the economies of the rest of the world need to grow more rapidly. But simply from the narrow objective of the sustainability of the current constellation of US growth and the value of the dollar, if other countries were to grow, the rate of return on their investments would rise and the US dollar would gradually depreciate as investors sought a broader mix in their portfolios of international assets instead of overweighting toward US dollar-denominated securities. Faster growth abroad and a drifting down of the dollar would naturally help to close the US current account gap. The longer growth in the rest of the world stagnates or remains slow, the longer foreign investors will choose US dollar-denominated assets and keep the dollar high, and the greater the potential for an unpleasant change in investor sentiment to affect the dollar, the United States, and the world.

References

Bank for International Settlements. 1998. Central Bank Survey of Foreign Exchange and Derivatives Market Activity. Basel: Bank for International Settlements.

Bayard, Thomas O., and Kimberly Ann Elliott. 1994. Reciprocity and Retaliation in U.S. Trade Policy. Washington: Institute for International Economics.

Baygan, Gunseli, and Catherine L. Mann. 1999. Technological Sophistication and Labor Productivity in the OECD. Washington: Institute for International Economics. Manuscript (January).

Bergsten, C. Fred. 1975. The Dilemmas of the Dollar: The Economics and Politics of United States International Monetary Policy. New York: New York University Press.

Bergsten, C. Fred. 1988. America in the World Economy: A Strategy for the 1990s. Washington: Institute for International Economics.

Bergsten, C. Fred. 1997. The Dollar and the Euro. Foreign Affairs 76, no. 4 (July-August): 83-95.

Bergsten, C. Fred, and Marcus Noland. 1993. Reconcilable Differences? United States–Japan Economic Conflict. Washington: Institute for International Economics.

Berman, Eli, John Bound, and Zvi Griliches. 1994. Changes in the Demand for Skilled Labor within U.S. Manufacturing Industries: Evidence from the Annual Survey of Manufactures. Quarterly Journal of Economics 109, no. 2 (May): 367-97.

Bernard, Andrew B., and J. Bradford Jensen. 1997. Exporters, Skill-Upgrading, and the Wage Gap. Journal of International Economics 42, no. 1-2 (February): 3-31.

Borjas, George, Richard Freeman, and Lawrence Katz. 1991. On the Labor Market Effects of Immigration and Trade. NBER Working Paper No. 3761. Cambridge, MA: National Bureau of Economic Research (June).

Borjas, George, and Valerie Ramey. 1993. Foreign Competition, Market Power, and Wage Inequality. NBER Working Paper No. 4556. Cambridge, MA: National Bureau of Economic Research (December).

Borjas, George, and Valerie Ramey. 1994. Time-Series Evidence on the Sources of Trends in Wage Inequality. American Economics Review 84, no. 2 (May): 10-16.

Bound, John, and George Johnson. 1992. Changes in the Structure of Wages in the 1980s: An Evaluation of Alternative Explanations. American Economics Review 82, no. 3 (June): 371-92.

Brauer, David A., and Susan Hickok. 1995. Explaining the Growing Inequality in Wages across Skill Levels. *Federal Reserve Board–New York Economic Policy Review* 1, no. 1 (January): 61-75.

Burtless, Gary. 1995. International Trade and the Rise in Earnings Inequalities. *Journal of Economic Literature* 33 (June): 800-16.

Claessens, Stijn, and Sudarshan Gooptu, eds. 1993. Portfolio Investment in Developing Countries. World Bank Discussion Paper No. 228. Washington: World Bank (December).

Cline, William R. 1989. *United States External Adjustment and the World Economy.* Washington: Institute for International Economics.

Cline, William R. 1997. *Trade and Income Distribution.* Washington: Institute for International Economics.

Collins, Susan. 1985. Technical Progress in a Three-Country Model with a Continuum of Goods. *Journal of International Economics* 19, no. 1-2 (August): 171-79.

Cooper, Richard. 1982. The Gold Standard: Historical Facts and Future Prospects. *Brookings Papers on Economic Activity* 1: 2-45.

Corrado, Carol, and Joe Mattey. 1997. Capacity Utilization. *Journal of Economic Perspectives* 11 (Winter): 151-67.

Corrado, Carol, and Lawrence Slifman. 1996. Decomposition of Productivity and Unit Costs. Occasional Staff Study No. 1. Washington: Federal Reserve Board of Governors (18 November).

Destler, I. M. 1995. *American Trade Politics,* 3d ed. Washington: Institute for International Economics, and New York: Twentieth Century Fund.

Durand, Martine, Christophe Madaschi, and Flavia Terribile. 1998. Trends in OECD Countries' International Competitiveness: The Influence of Emerging Market Economies. OECD Economics Department Working Paper No. 195. Paris: Organization for Economic Cooperation and Development.

Eichengreen, Barry. 1999. *Toward a New International Financial Architecture: A Practical Post-Asia Agenda.* Washington: Institute for International Economics.

Feenstra, Robert, and Gordon Hanson. 1995. Foreign Investment, Outsourcing, and Relative Wages. NBER Working Paper No. 5121. Cambridge, MA: National Bureau of Economic Research (May).

Feenstra, Robert, Wen Hai, Wing T. Woo, and Shunli Yao. 1998. The US–China Bilateral Trade Balance: Its Size and Determinants. NBER Working Paper No. W6598. Cambridge, MA: National Bureau of Economic Research (January).

Feketekuty, Geza. 1998. Setting the Agenda for the Next Round of Negotiations on Trade in Services. In *Launching New Global Trade Talks: An Action Agenda,* ed. Jeffrey J. Schott. Washington: Institute for International Economics.

Frankel, Allen B., and Catherine L. Mann. 1986. A Framework for Analyzing the Process of Financial Innovation. International Finance Discussion Working Paper No. 283. Washington: Federal Reserve Board of Governors (September).

Funabashi, Yoichi. 1989. *Managing the Dollar: From the Plaza to the Louvre,* 2d ed. Washington: Institute for International Economics.

Gale, William G., and John Sabelhaus. 1999. Perspectives on the Household Savings Rate. *Brookings Papers on Economic Activity* 1999:1 (forthcoming).

Garber, Peter M., and Lars E.O. Svensson. 1995. The Operation and Collapse of Fixed Exchange Rate Regimes. In *Handbook of International Economics,* vol. 3, ed. Gene M. Grossman and Kenneth Rogoff. New York: Elsevier, North-Holland.

Goldstein, Morris. 1998. *The Asian Financial Crisis: Causes, Cures, and Systemic Implications.* POLICY ANALYSES IN INTERNATIONAL ECONOMICS 55. Washington: Institute for International Economics.

Goldstein, Morris, Graciela Kaminsky, and Carmen Reinhart. Forthcoming. *Forecasting Financial Crises: Early Warning Indicators for Emerging Economies.* Washington: Institute for International Economics.

Gould, David. 1994. Immigrant Links to the Home Country: Empirical Implications for US Bilateral Trade Flows. *Review of Economics and Statistics* 76, no. 2 (May): 302-16.

Gordon, Robert J. 1999. Has the "New Economy" Rendered the Productivity Slowdown Obsolete? Northwestern University. Manuscript (14 June).

Graham, Edward M., and Paul R. Krugman. 1991. *Foreign Direct Investment in the United States*. Washington: Institute for International Economics.

Grubel, Herbert G. 1968. Internationally Diversified Portfolios: Welfare Gains and Capital Flows. *American Economic Review* 58, no. 4 (December): 1299-1314.

Hoekman, Bernard. 1995. Assessing the General Agreement on Trade in Services. In *The Uruguay Round and the Developing Economies*, ed. Will Martin and L. Alan Winters. World Bank Discussion Paper No. 307. Washington: World Bank.

Hooper, Peter, Karen Johnson, and Jaime Marquez. 1998. Trade Elasticities for G-7 Countries. International Finance Discussion Paper No. 609. Federal Reserve Board of Governors.

Hooper, Peter, and Catherine L. Mann. 1989. *The Emergence and Persistence of the US External Imbalance, 1980-1987*. Princeton Studies in International Finance No. 65. Princeton: Princeton University, Department of Economics, International Finance Section (October).

Hooper, Peter, with Elizabeth Vrankovich. 1997. International Comparisons of the Levels of Unit Labor Costs in Manufacturing. In *Quiet Pioneering: Robert M. Stern and His International Economic Legacy*, ed. Keith Maskus, Peter Hooper, Edward Leamer, and J. David Richardson. Ann Arbor, MI: University of Michigan Press. (Also available as International Finance Discussion Paper no. 527, Federal Reserve Board of Governors, October 1995.)

Houthakker, Hendrik S., and Stephen P. Magee. 1969. Income and Price Elasticities in World Trade. *Review of Economics and Statistics* 51: 111-25.

Katz, Lawrence, and Lawrence Summers. 1995. Industry Rents: Evidence and Implications. *Brookings Papers on Economic Activity: Microeconomics*. Washington: Brookings Institution.

Kletzer, Lori. 1998a. Job Displacement. *Journal of Economic Perspectives* 12, no. 1 (Winter): 115-36.

Kletzer, Lori. 1998b. Trade and Job Loss in US Manufacturing, 1975-1994. Working paper prepared for the NBER Conference on the Impact of International Trade on Wages (February).

Kravis, Irving B., and Robert E. Lipsey. 1988. The Competitiveness and Comparative Advantage of US Multinationals, 1957-1984. NBER Working Paper No. W2051. Cambridge, MA: National Bureau of Economic Research (October).

Krugman, Paul R. 1985. Is the Strong Dollar Sustainable? In *The U.S. Dollar: Recent Developments, Outlook, and Policy Options*. Federal Reserve Bank of Kansas City.

Krugman, Paul R. 1991. Has the Adjustment Process Worked? In *International Adjustment and Financing: The Lessons of 1985-1991*, ed. C. Fred Bergsten. Washington: Institute for International Economics.

Krugman, Paul R. 1997. Is Capitalism Too Productive? *Foreign Affairs* 76, no. 5 (September/October): 79-94.

Krugman, Paul R., and Robert Lawrence. 1996. Trade, Wages, and Jobs. In *Pop Internationalism*, ed. Paul R. Krugman. Cambridge, MA: MIT Press.

Kurian, George Thomas. 1994. *Datapedia of the United States, 1790-2000: America Year By Year*. Lanham, MD: Bernan Press.

Leamer, Edward. 1994. Trade, Wages, and Revolving Door Ideas. NBER Working Paper No. 4716. Cambridge, MA: National Bureau of Economic Research (April).

Levich, Richard M. 1998. *International Financial Markets: Prices and Policies*. Boston: Irwin/McGraw-Hill.

Lewis, Karen K. 1995. Puzzles in International Financial Markets. In *The Handbook of International Economics*, vol. 3, ed. Gene Grossman and Kenneth Rogoff. New York: Elsevier, North-Holland.

Lewis, Karen K. 1999. Trying to Explain Home Bias in Equities and Consumption. *Journal of Economic Literature* 37, no. 2 (June 1999): 571-608.

Lipsey, Robert E. 1991. Foreign Direct Investment in the United States and US Trade. *Annals of the American Academy of Political and Social Science* 516: 76-90.

Lyons, Richard. 1995. Tests of Microstructural Hypotheses in the Foreign Exchange Market. *Journal of Financial Economics* 39, no. 2-3 (October): 321-51.

Mankiw, Gregory. 1997. *Macroeconomics*, 3d ed. New York: Worth Publishers.

Mann, Catherine L. 1986. Price, Profit Margins, and Exchange Rates. *Federal Reserve Bulletin* 72, no. 6 (June).

Mann, Catherine L. 1988. The Effect of Foreign Competition in Prices and Quantities on Employment in Import-Sensitive U.S. Industries. *International Trade Journal* 2, no. 4 (Summer): 409-44.

Mann, Catherine L. 1991. Structural Change and Prospects for Sustained Improvement in the U.S. External Balance. *Contemporary Policy Issues* 9, no. 2 (April): 50-58.

Mann, Catherine L. 1996. Exchange Rates, Import Prices, and Inflation: A Missing Link? Washington: Federal Reserve Board of Governors. Manuscript.

Mann, Catherine L. 1997. Trade, Technology, and the American Worker. Washington: Institute for International Economics. Manuscript (December; revised August 1998).

Mann, Catherine L. 1998. Globalization and Productivity Growth in the United States and Germany. In *Globalization, Technological Change, and Labor Markets*, ed. Stanley W. Black. Boston: Kluwer Academic Publishers.

Mann, Catherine L. 1999. Market Mechanisms to Reduce the Need for IMF Bailouts. International Economics Policy Briefs No. 99-4 (February). Washington: Institute for International Economics.

Marquez, Jaime. 1990. Bilateral Trade Elasticities. *Review of Economics and Statistics* 72, no. 1 (February): 70-77.

Marquez, Jaime. 1998. The Elasticity Puzzle in US Imports and the Role of Demographic Factors. Washington: Federal Reserve Board of Governors. Manuscript (July).

Marquez, Jaime. 1999. Immigration and US Imports. Washington: Federal Reserve Board of Governors. Manuscript (25 January).

Marris, Stephen. 1985. *Deficits and the Dollar: The World Economy at Risk*. POLICY ANALYSES IN INTERNATIONAL ECONOMICS 14. Washington: Institute for International Economics.

McKinsey Global Institute. 1992. *Services Sector Productivity*. Washington: McKinsey Global Institute (October).

Merrill Lynch. 1998. *Size and Structure of the World Bond Market, 1998*. New York: Merrill Lynch (September).

Milesi-Ferretti, Gian Maria, and Assarf Razin. 1996. *Current Account Sustainability*. Princeton Studies in International Finance No. 81. Princeton: Princeton University, Department of Economics, International Finance Section (October).

Murphy, Kevin, and Finis Welch. 1991. Wage Differentials in the 1980s: The Role of International Trade. In *Workers and Their Wages*, ed. Marvin Kosters. Washington: American Enterprise Institute Press.

Murphy, Kevin, and Finis Welch. 1992. The Structure of Wages. *Quarterly Journal of Economics* 107, no. 1 (February): 285-326.

Noland, Marcus, Sherman Robinson, and Zhi Wang. 1999. The Continuing Asian Financial Crisis: Global Adjustment and Trade. Working Paper Series No. 99-4. Washington: Institute for International Economics.

Obstfeld, Maurice, and Kenneth Rogoff. 1995. The Intertemporal Approach to the Current Account. In *The Handbook of International Economics*, vol. 3, ed. Gene Grossman and Kenneth Rogoff. New York: Elsevier, North-Holland.

Organization for Economic Cooperation and Development (OECD). 1996. *OECD Jobs Study*. Paris: OECD.

Organization for Economic Cooperation and Development (OECD). 1997. *The World in 2020: Towards a New Global Age*. Paris: OECD.

Organization for Economic Cooperation and Development (OECD). 1998a. Measuring Electronic Commerce: International Trade in Software. Working Party on the Information Economy, DTSI/ICCP/IE(98)3/Final (30 April).

Organization for Economic Cooperation and Development (OECD). 1998b. *Fostering Entrepreneurship*. Paris: OECD.

Organization for Economic Cooperation and Development (OECD). 1998c. *Education at a Glance: OECD Indicators 1998*. Paris: OECD, Centre for Educational Research Innovation.

Preeg, Ernest H. 1998. The U.S. Trillion Dollar Debt to Foreign Central Banks. Second Prize Essay in the 1998 Essay Competition in honor of Jacques de Larosière. Washington: Institute of International Finance (September).

Richardson, J. David. 1995. Income Inequality and Trade: How to Think, What to Conclude. *Journal of Economic Perspectives* 9, no. 3 (Summer): 33-55.

Richardson, J. David, and Karin Rindal. 1995. *Why Exports Really Matter!* Washington: Institute for International Economics and the Manufacturing Institute (July).

Richardson, J. David, and Karin Rindal. 1996. *Why Exports Matter: More!* Washington: Institute for International Economics and the Manufacturing Institute (February).

Rosen, Daniel H. 1999. China and the World Trade Organization: An Economic Balance Sheet. International Economics Policy Briefs No. 99-6 (June). Washington: Institute for International Economics.

Schott, Jeffrey J., with Johanna W. Buurman. 1994. *The Uruguay Round: An Assessment*. Washington: Institute for International Economics.

Schott, Jeffrey J. 1996. *The World Trading System: Challenges Ahead*. Washington: Institute for International Economics.

Sekiguchi, David. 1997. Some Simple Current Account Arithmetics. New York: J. P. Morgan Securities, Emerging Markets Research (6 June).

Sichel, Daniel E. 1999. Computers and Aggregate Economic Growth: An Update. *Business Economics* 34, no. 2 (April): 18-24.

Snape, Richard H., and Malcolm Bosworth. 1996. Advancing Services Negotiations. In *The World Trading System: Challenges Ahead*, ed. Jeffrey J. Schott. Washington: Institute for International Economics.

Stevens, Guy V.G. 1997. U.S. International Transactions in 1996. *Federal Reserve Bulletin*. Washington: Board of Governors of the Federal Reserve (May).

Summers, Robert, and Alan Heston. 1991. The Penn World Table (Mark 5): An Expanded Set of International Comparisons, 1950-1988. *Quarterly Journal of Economics* 106, no. 2 (May): 327-68.

Triffin, Robert. 1960. *Gold and the Dollar Crisis*. New Haven, CT: Yale University Press.

Warner, Andrew. 1998a. Income Distribution and Competitiveness. In *Global Competitiveness Report 1998*. Lausanne, Switzerland: World Economic Forum.

Warner, Andrew. 1998b. Methodology. In *Global Competitiveness Report 1998*. Lausanne, Switzerland: World Economic Forum.

Wood, Adrian. 1995. How Trade Hurt Unskilled Workers. *Journal of Economic Perspectives* 9, no. 3 (Summer): 57-80.

World Bank. 1999. *Global Commodity Markets: A Comprehensive Review and Price Forecast*. Washington: World Bank (January).

World Economic Forum. 1998. *Global Competitiveness Report 1998*. Lausanne, Switzerland: World Economic Forum.

Wren-Lewis, Simon, and Rebecca L. Driver. 1998. *Real Exchange Rates for the Year 2000*. POLICY ANALYSES IN INTERNATIONAL ECONOMICS 54. Washington: Institute for International Economics.

Index

and productivity growth, 57–59
and relative prices, 100
Wealth
  financial, globalization of, 148
  personal, 21, 22*f*
Wealth portfolios, global, and deficit
    sustainability, 150

World Economic Forum, 95, 110, 110*n*, 111,
    111*n*
World Trade Organization, 84*n*–85*n*
Wren-Lewis, Simon, 168

Yochelson, John, 95

Other Publications from the
Institute for International Economics

POLICY ANALYSES IN INTERNATIONAL ECONOMICS Series

SPECIAL REPORTS

WORKS IN PROGRESS

Explaining Congressional Votes on Recent Trade Bills:
From NAFTA to Fast Track
Robert E. Baldwin and Christopher S. Magee
The New Politics of American Trade
Peter J. Balint and I.M. Destler
The US - Japan Economic Relationship
C. Fred Bergsten, Marcus Noland, and Takatoshi Ito
China's Entry to the World Economy
Richard N. Cooper
Reforming Economic Sanctions
Kimberly Ann Elliott, Gary C. Hufbauer and Jeffrey J. Schott
Leading Indicators of Financial Crises in the Emerging Economies
Morris Goldstein and Carmen Reinhart
The Failure of MAI Negotiations and Prospects for the Future
Edward M. Graham
Prospects for Western Hemisphere Free Trade
Gary Clyde Hufbauer and Jeffrey J. Schott
The Future of US Foreign Aid
Carol Lancaster
Measuring the Costs of Protection in Europe
Patrick Messerlin
The Economics of Korean Unification
Marcus Noland
International Lender of Last Resort
Catherine L. Mann
Globalization, the NAIRU, and Monetary Policy
Adam S. Posen
Germany in the World Economy after the EMU
Adam S. Posen
Prospects for Western Hemisphere Free Trade
Jeffrey J. Schott
India in the World Economy
T.N. Srinivasan and Suresh D. Tendulkar

DISTRIBUTORS OUTSIDE THE UNITED STATES

Australia, New Zealand, and
Papua New Guinea
D.A. INFORMATION SERVICES
648 Whitehorse Road
Mitcham, Victoria 3132, Australia
(tel: 61-3-9210-7777;
fax: 61-3-9210-7788)
email: service@dadirect.com.au
http://www.dadirect.com.au

Canada
RENOUF BOOKSTORE
5369 Canotek Road, Unit 1,
Ottawa, Ontario K1J 9J3, Canada
(tel: 613-745-2665;
fax: 613-745-7660)
http://www.renoufbooks.com

Central America, and the Caribbean
(non-anglophone islands only)
Jose Rios, sales representative
Publishers Marketing & Research Associates
Publicaciones Educativas
Apartado Postal 370-A
Ciudad Guatemala, GUATEMALA, C.A.
(phone/fax 502-443-0472)

Colombia, Ecuador, and Peru
Infoenlace Ltda
Attn: Octavio Rojas
Calle 72 No. 13-23 Piso 3
Edificio Nueva Granada, Bogota, D.C.
Colombia
(tel. (571) 255 8783 or 255 7969
fax (571) 248 0808 or 217 6435)

India, Bangladesh, Nepal, and Sri Lanka
Viva Books Pvt.
Mr. Vinod Vasishtha
4325/3, Ansari Rd.
Daryaganj, New Delhi-110002
INDIA
(tel: 91-11-327-9280
fax: 91-11-326-7224)
email:
vinod.viva@gndel.globalnet.ems.vsnl.net.in

Northern Africa and The Middle East
(Egypt, Algeria, Bahrain, Palestine, Jordan,
Kuwait, Lebanon, Libya, Morocco, Oman,
Qatar, Saudi Arabia, Syria, Tunisia, Yemen,
and United Arab Emirates)
The Middle East Observer
41 Sherif Street
Cairo, Egypt
(phone (202) 392-6919; fax (202) 3939-732)
e-mail: mafouda@meobserver.com.eg

South America
Julio E. Emod
Publishers Marketing & Research Associates,
c/o HARBRA
Rua Joaquim Tavora, 629
04015-001 Sao Paulo, Brasil
(phone (55) 11-571-1122; fax (55) 11-575-6876)
e-mail: emod@harbra.com.br

Argentina
World Publications SA.
Av. Cordoba 1877
1120 Buenos Aires, Argentina
(tel/fax: (54 11) 4815 8156)
email: wpbooks@infovia.com.ar

Caribbean
SYSTEMATICS STUDIES LIMITED
St. Augustine Shopping Centre
Eastern Main Road, St. Augustine
Trinidad and Tobago, West Indies
(tel: 868-645-8466;
fax: 868-645-8467)
email: tobe@trinidad.net

People's Republic of China (including Hong
Kong) **and Taiwan** (sales representatives):
Tom Cassidy
Cassidy & Associates
70 Battery Place, Ste 220
New York, NY 10280
(tel: 212-706-2200; fax: 212-706-2254)
email: CHINACAS@Prodigy.net

United Kingdom and Europe (including Russia
and Turkey)
The Eurospan Group
3 Henrietta Street, Covent Garden
London WC2E 8LU England
Visit their website and order via their "secure
order form". Alternatively call their customer
services line on 44-20-7240-0856, or fax to
44-20-7379-0609. Customers in the UK must dial
a (0) before the city code (20).

Japan and the Republic of Korea
United Publishers Services, Ltd.
Kenkyu-Sha Bldg.
9, Kanda Surugadai 2-Chome
Chiyoda-Ku, Tokyo 101
JAPAN
(tel: 81-3-3291-4541; fax: 81-3-3292-8610)
email: saito@ups.co.jp

South Africa
Pat Bennink
Dryad Books
PO Box 11684
Vorna Valley 1686
South Africa
(tel: +27 11 805 6019;
fax: +27 11 805 3746)
email: dryad@hixnet.co.za

Taiwan
Unifacmanu Trading Co., Ltd.
4F, No.91, Ho-Ping East Road, Section 1,
Taipei 10609, Taiwan
(phone 886-2-23419646; fax 886-2-23943103)
e-mail: winjoin@ms12.hinet.net

Visit our website at: http://www.iie.com E-mail orders to: orders@iie.com